The Recovery of a

Woman Sailor

NANCY WROE

ISBN 978-1-0980-6409-9 (paperback)
ISBN 978-1-0980-6410-5 (digital)

Christian Faith Publishing, Inc.
832 Park Avenue
Meadville, PA 16335
www.christianfaithpublishing.com

Printed in the United States of America

Chapter 1

Life Before the Navy

As I was walking up the gangplank to my new home, the USS *Shenandoah*, I was thinking of what someone had told me earlier, that those repair ships were tied to the pier, which means they don't go out to sea very often. But as I got to the quarterdeck, the sailor on watch checked my ID, looked me in the eye, and said, "Expect to be in port just one month in the next year and a half." I was somewhat excited since that's what I joined the Navy to do, "sail on ships." Probably because I grew up the daughter of a Navy sailor, and I was always fascinated with big ships and loved being on the water. I had just reenlisted after four years of shore duty, and this was supposed to be my duty station for the next six years. Unfortunately, it would take me away from my daughter and husband; but I knew that was part of military life, like my dad when he was away most of my life growing up. I can't complain, though, because my first enlistment, all shore duty, was more than I could ever imagine. I joined the Navy for a better life for me and my daughter, and my first objective was to bowl for the Navy on the All-Navy Bowling team, which was a dream come true.

I was born in Balboa Naval Hospital in San Diego, California. My dad was a submariner in the Navy and recently retired around the time I was born. He decided to try his hand at pool maintenance, but it must not have been enough money to take care of five children, or he missed being on the water. Then he got word that they were building a ship for the Coast and Geodetic Survey, which is now called NOAA, and they needed a quartermaster, which was his job in the Navy. After talking it over with mom, he enlisted. Unfortunately, after it was built, it was destined to be stationed in Seattle, Washington. I say unfortunately because I was enjoying life all too well in the desert in El Cajon, a suburb of San Diego, till I was around eight years old when we moved to Seattle.

When I was only five or six years old, my dad took us kids on a hike up on a hill near where we lived. As we got near the top of the mountain, or hill, my dad saw a rattlesnake on the trail. He told my sister and me to get behind the rocks, then he and my brothers got a couple of forked sticks and tied the head and tail of the snake to them. We then carried the snake down the mountain to our house. My dad called the San Diego Zoo and gave the snake to them. It turned out to be the biggest diamondback rattlesnake they ever had and put him on display till he died. My Dad taught us to respect all wildlife, not to fear it. I never ever wanted my life there to change, especially moving far away. But it eventually did.

My dad was a remarkable man and lived an incredible life, but the story of his father was equally intriguing. My dad never talked a lot about his own life and he wasn't home enough to be able to communicate with us kids a lot either. If we wanted to know something, we had to practically pry it out of him. I got bits and pieces from my big brother, Gary, or my uncle Ted, who lived in Cody, Wyoming, till he died in 2018. This is what I've learned. My grandfather, Elmer Lee, was a sharecropper and traveled all around the country working on big farms alongside former slaves and children of slaves, but he never considered himself better than they were. He eventually moved to Cody, Wyoming, where he met my grandmother, Carrie. They were married in Yellowstone Park in 1912. Soon after marriage, he heard a story about a steamboat captain, Grant Marsh, in the 1870s, and one of the greatest unclaimed treasures in history. Just after the civil war in June of 1876, he, the steamboat captain, was carrying $370,000 worth of gold (which is worth over eight million today) up the Missouri River from the gold miners down river. He heard that they needed help to get the wounded, at Custer's Last Stand, to a hospital 700 miles away, but his boat could only hold fifty wounded and he had to unload the gold because the river was too shallow. He decided to bury the gold on the riverbank on the Little Big Horn River, but when he came back for it, he couldn't find it or where he buried it. Nobody knows what happened to the gold.

Because of my grandfather's wanderlust and was enticed by the prospect of finding this treasure, he packed up and moved himself and his new wife to the Little Big Horn in Montana. He worked out a deal with the Crow Indians to buy some property right near Custer's Last Stand on the reservation. I don't know how he did it because not very many white men were allowed to buy property on reservations, even now. He then constructed his own house, and being knowledgeable about cement, he built it on a cement slab. This house stood until it was demolished sometime in the 1980s. In 1914, two days before Christmas, Carrie was in labor with my dad, Gilbert. Elmer hooked up the buckboard to the horses to take her to the doctor, but when they got to the river, they noticed an Indian on the other side, waving his hands. He was trying to let them know that the river was moving too fast to go across. Because he wasn't sure he got his message through to them, he rode his horse into the river and got swept downstream. The Indian and his horse survived, but he risked his life to let them know not to cross that river. My grandparents immediately turned the wagon around and went back to the reservation where my father was born on Christmas Eve. I figured he was born at the Little Big Horn only thirty eight years after Custer's Last Stand. Since my grandfather couldn't find the gold, he moved back to Cody, Wyoming, where he got a job driving a stagecoach through Yellowstone Park till 1917 when internal combustion engines in busses took over. My uncle Ted says he was also good friends with William "Buffalo Bill" Cody. I remember seeing my grandmother, Carrie, in 1967 in Cody, Wyoming, when we took a trip around the United States. I was only thirteen years old at the time. I didn't know too much about her background except that she was a Norwegian, born from Norwegian immigrants and a good Christian Presbyterian. She said she read the Bible daily. I was always impressed with that. I know that she had a big influence on my dad as a Christian; even Uncle Ted went to church until he had to be put in a nursing home, right before he died. I'm very proud to say that there is a monument in Cody, Wyoming, for my grandparents, Elmer and Carrie Lee, in honor of all five of their sons going to war in WW2 and coming home safe. Each of them has a plaque with their names engraved with their rank and military assignment.

Elmer and Carrie Lee

Elmer and Carrie Lee 5 sons WW2 Memorial

WW2 monument in Cody WY

My dad, Gilbert F. Lee, served in WW2 on a submarine, called the USS F Flounder, which was the only US submarine to destroy a German Sub or U-Boat in the western hemisphere. The Flounder also sank a Japanese troop ship which helped change the balance of the war at that time. The story of this submarine was actually told on a television show in the late 50s called The Silent Service.

His brother, Ted Lee was in the Army's 82nd Airborne Division and one of his jobs during WW2 was a guard outside the office of Dwight D. Eisenhower in Germany.

Then on my mother's side of the family, Mom and all four of her sisters went to an all girls' school in Groton, Connecticut. It happened to be near the Navy submarine school where Dad was going. That's where they met and soon got married. Her sisters also met their soon-to-be husbands there. My mother's sister, Jesse, enlisted in the Navy as a nurse, but when she married her husband, who was also a naval officer, they would not allow them both to stay in together, so she got out of the Navy and enlisted in the army as a nurse.

Jessie Petrat in uniform 1941

The move to Seattle

You would think that moving to a place where living on the tallest hill, called Queen Anne Hill, and watching the Space Needle being built right before the World's Fair began, would be exciting; but for an eight-year-old child forced to make the climb in the back seat of the car up a hill, the local people, called Seattlites, nicknamed "the counterbalance." I understood why they called it that because it was so steep. In the back seat of the car it felt like we were going to fall backward. It was so traumatic, I remember feeling like I was in a bubble as we went up that hill for the first time. Maybe it was a way of feeling protected, like a force field or something. Later, I started hiding in the closet when I wasn't getting enough attention. My parents took me and my brother and sister up in the Space Needle, which was so frightening, I started wetting my pants. Going from a warm, dry climate, "the desert," to, of course, cold and rainy typical Seattle weather wasn't very nice either. When we moved, we left our dog behind too, a beautiful collie named Princey Boy; and my elder brother and sister ran off and got married. My sister was like a mother to me, which made me feel abandoned when she left. Because of this, my brother, who was only four years older than me, took my elder sister's place and became mine and my younger sister's caretaker or babysitter, which was horrible since he was only twelve years old and loved punching us in the arm and constantly teasing us.

My mother always depended on kids taking care of kids because she liked her time not doing it herself. There were times when I didn't think she really liked kids at all, but she had to be an incredible mother raising five kids, most of the time all by herself since Dad was gone to war and didn't even see his firstborn son until after he was two years old. Then when she thought he was retired, he started a new job for the government, on surface ships, and was gone again for months at a time. She was also a very talented musician and played several instruments such as the tuba, piano, and organ, just to name a few. I know I got my musical gene from her like my brother Gary who played the trumpet. My mother was also so good with finances that we never went without food and no hand-me-downs either on just my father's income. Every year, right before school started, we would go shopping for new clothes. I always loved that time of year. That's pretty good for being a stay-at-home mom and living on a military or government fixed income. She was also a fantastic cook, and because all the kids learned from her, both brothers became great chefs. Gary left home at sixteen to become a fireman and started cooking for the San Diego Fire Department to get on the payroll because he was so young. He also graduated high school and got married at that age. My other brother Rick, at age eighteen, became a chef for King Oscars, the restaurant where the mayor of Seattle had his daughter's wedding reception. That's how nice it was.

We first lived in Seattle on Queen Anne Hill for three years and moved right around the corner from the Presbyterian church, where we went to church by going out our back door to Sunday school class. Very convenient. This was the only time growing up that I remember going to church. My mom even sang in the choir. My dad would teach us prayers when we went to bed at night. In spite of the traumatic experiences, this time in my life was a great lesson, learning about the love of Jesus in Sunday school. I remember looking at a picture of Jesus on the wall and saying to myself, "At least Jesus loves me." I was going through a time when I felt very insecure, and my dad was gone a lot, and when he came home, it seemed we were in competition for his love and attention. Suddenly, I became a middle child. Then my brother would teach us about the life of hard knocks by taking us to the movies, usually James Bond and horror movies, and to the woods where he would teach us about sex by kissing girls. He became a big part of my growing up.

The move to Birch Bay

One summer, my parents bought a travel trailer; and we took a vacation north to a trailer park in Birch Bay, Washington. It was right on the coast, just eight miles south of the Canadian border. We stayed two weeks. After we got home, our parents asked us if we wanted to live there. Of course we said yes! So we bought the trailer park and called it Lee's Trailer Terrace. It became the best time of my entire life, which lasted three whole years. I was only ten, but I started to grow up with more responsibilities and more freedom than most grown-ups ever have. I always loved horses, so of course I discovered the riding stables and spent most of my free time there working as a stable hand and taking groups of vacationers out on trail rides. I had my own horse that I named Wahoo. My best friend, Maryland, named her horse Wahelo. Mr. Meador was the owner and took advantage of the free help, even though we were only children. That would be unheard of in today's world. I also worked at the roller rink blowing the whistle at people speeding around the rink too fast. I had my home responsibilities too, where I would act as a lifeguard at our pool and help sell ceramics in our own shop. My mother bought a kiln because she always loved making ceramics. This was a dream of hers to have her own shop. My brother would keep the lawn mowed. There were times, not very often, I would be left home alone and would park trailers that would come in. I also worked making my own money in the strawberry fields. That was my first actual job. I was only ten years old when I learned the value of money and how to save. We would be picked up by a bus and taken to the fields to pick strawberries all day and then be taken home. One day, I remember well, I picked a whole flat, which was about half a day's picking, and walked around the corner to go to the restroom. When I got back, they were gone. I learned I had to get paid first for the strawberries before I went to the bathroom. It was an expensive lesson.

My brother had two .22 rifles and let me hunt rabbits with him in the fields across the street. I also got a bow and some arrows for Christmas one year and went rabbit hunting with that too. I learned how to skin the rabbits to make the pelts nice and soft with rocks and salt just like the Native Americans.

During the winter, or off season, the horses at the riding stables would be grazing in the fields, which happened to be across the street from where we lived. I would go over and jump on my horse, Wahoo, and pretend I was an Indian, riding around the fields with the other horses. Mr. Meader never knew it, but one day, I went over to see the hoses and found them loose in the middle of the road, so I rounded them up and got them inside the field and fixed the fence. It was a good thing I kept an eye on them, but I loved doing it. I think caring for people and animals stayed with me all my life.

We even had a recreation room in the lower half of the house with pool tables and pinball machines. I learned early how to make a hustle. One of our neighbors had a motorcycle, and he taught me how to ride it, in spite of crashing a few times at first. I kept letting out the clutch too fast. I finally got it right and rode for years later.

My best friend and I even became patrols on our school bus. Like security guards, our job was to ensure safety, making sure everyone was seated when we were moving, and no fights erupted. It was hard since the high school kids always sat in the back of the bus, making it their domain, and we were not welcome, especially the senior boys. The first time I went back there, a big boy grabbed me by the waist, and holding my arms together so I couldn't move, he put me on his lap and everybody started laughing. I wasn't amused. In fact, after he let me go, I asked the bus driver, Mr. Glen, if I could have permission to slap him. He said, "Yes." Needless to say, I walked back there again and he did the same thing, grabbing me and putting me on his lap. I relaxed my arms and he relaxed his grip, and I pulled my arm back and I slapped him. Pretty hard too. Because he was so startled, he grabbed my arms again and asked, "If I let you go, would you not hit me again?" I said, "Yes, but you have to promise me not to cause any more trouble." He agreed, and he slowly put me down in the aisle, and I never had to go back there again. The thing I noticed about my attitude with life, at this time, was that I wasn't intimidated or fearful. That later changed, unfortunately.

I loved school also, especially physical education. It wasn't easy either. We did a lot of running and climbing ropes, which were my favorite things to do. I heard that this school sent a few people to the Olympics and I can understand why. I liked English class too. I even won a spelling bee in elementary school.

One year our school went to the Peace Arch Park and sat down on the grass to hear President Johnson speak about making peace with the Canadians because they were crossing the border and looting the businesses on the US side in Blaine, Washington. I think it was in protest of getting involved in Vietnam at the time. It was around 1965 that this happened.

Back to Seattle

Then after three years of living a life most people just dream about, we moved back to Seattle. It was a big adjustment, moving from the country to the city, to the country, and then back to the city. I hated Seattle. It was usually cold and wet, and I got used to horseback riding and roller-skating at the local roller rink in Birch Bay. It was hard, especially being at age thirteen. In fact, when I went to school, in my first class, a boy from the back of the class called out, "Hey, turtle head," because I had very short hair, and they said I looked like a turtle. From then on, I stopped cutting my hair and let it grow. For the next three years, I was constantly teased and bullied, but they didn't call it bullying back then. Because I was small and skinny, with a pixie haircut, giving me that turtle-head look, the bigger girls always wanted to beat me up, but I had too much pride, and I never wanted to back down. To defend myself, I would tell them I'd meet them on the playground after school, and then I found out right away I was usually faster than they were and ran away. I got into about eight fights a year for the next three years. I never told my parents because I thought I'd get in trouble, so I learned to keep my feelings inside even though I was terrified, and I never cried because I learned from my brother that that was a sign of weakness. Soon after moving to Seattle, my parents, who liked bowling themselves, took me to the bowling alley; and I joined a league on Saturday mornings. It seemed I was a natural athlete, and my second year bowling I almost had a perfect game, 268. Every ball was in the pocket, but my ball was so light (just ten pounds), I got all the pins down except I left one pin standing only twice out of twelve frames.

When I was fourteen, I went to a wedding for one of my bowling teammates, who was a lot older than I was, and I discovered champagne at the reception. I immediately fell in love with that feeling of euphoria it gave me. Unfortunately, from then on alcohol became the great obsession of my life and my trying to escape from life.

At age fifteen, I tried out and made the Seattle Junior All-Stars. We bowled against other cities in Washington State. If you know anything about bowling, Earl Anthony was, and still is, considered the top bowler in the world; and he bowled on the Tacoma All-Stars. He also coached me a few times. I had a dream that someday I would bowl in the Olympics, even though bowling wasn't even in the Olympics yet.

When I wasn't bowling, all I could think about was my next drink, and I would go out drinking on Friday nights and come in on Saturday mornings to the junior league. I would go out with a decent boyfriend who didn't really drink much but let me drink all I wanted to, and I would bowl the next day with a hangover. They all knew I was drinking a lot, and my teammates nicknamed me Fish. I pretty much did that, off and on, through high school, depending on what kind of boyfriend I had. In fact, I would have won a scholarship in the state tournament in my senior year, but my grades weren't good enough, and I know that was probably because of my drinking. I only had a C grade average, and I knew I could have done much better if only I had applied myself. I didn't like school because of the teasing. After my parents first saw me drunk at the wedding, I felt so embarrassed that I promised myself that they would never see me drunk again. And I kept my promise. My brother Rick had a ski boat, and we'd go out water-skiing on weekends, and as long as our parents weren't with us, he would buy a case of beer, and I'd usually end up sitting on the bank, just drinking the beer. When we got home, I would sneak in the house and crawl up the stairs and into bed so my parents wouldn't catch me.

I let my parents think they had a perfect child, and since my mother was a musician, I learned to play the drums and became a musician. I was in five classes of music in junior high school, and when I got to high school, I made top drummer. I also played in the All-City Band and All-City Orchestra and played the timpani and percussion in the Seattle Opera House. My high school marching band got invited to play in a parade in Victoria, British Columbia, for Queen Elizabeth's birthday. We were right between the Queen and the Guess Who, a Canadian rock band. So far, in my life, I've seen two famous people, President Johnson and Queen Elizabeth, in person.

I had a good friend who became my best friend all through high school. Her name was Renae. She helped me a lot because all the time I spent around her and her family, I didn't drink or even think about a drink because they looked down on it. Renae was my best friend in the world, but her stepdad thought we were too close and accused us of being lesbians, but we just laughed at that because we were too interested in boys at the time. My parents weren't too keen on my spending too much time at her house either, but I didn't feel I could talk to my parents at the time about personal things going on in my life. I was a typical teenager going through puberty, feeling very awkward and lonely.

Heading to the Seattle Opera House

Renae had two brothers, Larry and Gary. I could tell that her brother Gary (the older one) had a crush on me because when we were walking one day, he took a hold of my hand. He didn't say anything, but I hated to tell him I didn't feel that way for him. He seemed more like a brother to me. I thought he was too old for me anyway. He was twenty-nine, and I was seventeen at the time. Her mother treated me like another daughter also. She was a Norwegian, and my grandmother on my father's side was Norwegian. She made the best Norwegian potato pancakes called lefse. The Norwegian language was being taught in our school that year, and we decided to take the class so we could communicate with her mother in her native tongue. Renae's father was Swedish but died when she was a baby, so that made her half Swedish and half Norwegian. I also took two years of French because my mother was half French and half English.

Renae loved the outdoors as much as I did, so we both joined the hiking club together. We had a wonderful teacher, Mr. Jones, who took us on hikes around the state of Washington. One weekend we started at the base of Mount Rainier and hiked about ten miles into the woods to a place called Kennedy Hot Springs, where the volcanic activity of Mount Rainier was apparent. We spent the night in our sleeping bags on the bare ground, without a tent, under the stars. The temperature literally got down into the upper thirties. I thought we were going to freeze to death. Some of the kids jumped into the hot springs with just their underwear. During the night, we all huddled as close as possible to the fire and to each other to keep warm.

This is the way I grew up, with my dad taking us, my brother and sister and me, in the middle of the night, rain or shine, no matter what the weather, out camping and fishing. I seem to remember it being mostly cold and rainy. That was the average weather of the Pacific Northwest.

One day, Mr. Jones, our hiking club teacher, and his girlfriend, climbed to the top of Mount Rainier. When he made the summit, over 14,000 feet up, he proposed to her on the top. On the way down, he slipped and fell down into a crevasse. His body was never found. It was a horrible tragedy, and I remember going to the memorial service. Our music teacher, who encouraged me to learn to play the drums, had a beautiful voice and sang for him. The hiking club disbanded after that, but Renae and I stayed best friends till we graduated high school.

CHAPTER 2
MY CLOSE ENCOUNTER

Gary, Renae's brother, bought some property in Eastern Washington. It was out in the middle of nowhere at the base of the Cascades near the Canadian border, and it had two cabins on it. One cabin was a large empty log cabin right next to another cabin with two bedrooms with bunk beds and a dining room with a table where we ate and played cards in the evenings. There was no water or electricity in the cabins. We went there three summers in a row. The first two summers we stayed two weeks, and nothing unusual happened. This was going to be the last time we went, which was just before our senior year; but with the circumstances that were going to affect me for the rest of my life, we only stayed one week.

As we left Seattle to go on our summer vacation in Eastern Washington, Renae and I were tucked in the back of the pickup between two motorcycles heading for their two cabins located on the Lost River.

It was about a twenty-four-hour trip to Eastern Washington and not too comfortable, but lying on blankets and pillows, we made the best of it and slept most of the way through the mountains and Snoqualmie Pass. Thank goodness it was summer, and the weather was beautiful and not too cold this time of year, but we did have to bundle up as we were going through the mountain pass. When we got to the other side, it was very dry like a desert, but that's normal in Eastern Washington, unlike Seattle, where it rains a lot. Not too many people know that Washington State has more weather conditions than any other state in the union; and where we were going, it's considered a desert area, with a mixture of ponderosa pines and fields of waist-high yellow grass. Beautiful country, in my opinion. On the other hand, on the western side of Seattle is the Olympic Peninsula where it's considered a rain forest, with a couple hundred inches of rain a year. Big contrast.

Gary and Larry were taking turns driving all night and half the day when we finally drove into Mazama, a quiet little town consisting of only two people, a husband and wife. It had a general store and a single old-fashioned gasoline pump. You had to actually pump the gas by hand. After pumping gas into the pickup truck, we were off to the cabin, which was getting closer, but it was still another ten miles on the dirt road. When we got to the driveway, which was almost another mile long, we had to get out in front of the pickup and move big boulders left by rock slides during the winter. As we neared the cabin, we were kinda perplexed. As we got closer, we wondered where the river was, because the first two times we were there, there was a rushing river about fifty feet in front of the cabin. The appropriately named Lost River has changed its course and this year went underground right in front of the cabins. Sounds unusual, but that's not the only unusual thing that was in store for us.

Once we got there, even though we were extremely tired from the long trip, we were all eager to get things put away and the beds made before the sun went down. After getting unpacked, we made sandwiches for dinner that evening; but before we went to bed, we wanted to stay up and play cards. That was a typical pastime activity we did even at home. The sun had just passed the horizon when I noticed the dead silence. No crickets, no birds...nothing. Suddenly, we heard a noise just outside the front door like a tin can being kicked. We looked at one another, not saying a word.

I broke the silence and said, "Gary, would you go out and see what that noise was?"

He said, "Let's wait till morning when it's light out." Of course, he was scared. We all were. We decided to go to bed and worry about it in the morning.

The next morning, still wondering what that noise was, I walked outside; and looking to the left by the side of the house, I saw an empty gasoline can on its side. I figured a raccoon or some other small animal was playing around and knocked it over. I turned to the right to walk around the other corner of the house and noticed a stinky smell filling the air. I looked down and saw a headless pheasant. The body was still fresh, with flies around the top of the neck where the head was missing. At first, I thought Larry was playing a joke, but he's more of a pacifist like his brother and wouldn't kill a fly. And what about the gas can? I asked Larry about it, and he just said, "Don't look at me. I didn't do anything." I believed him. We all wondered what on earth would do such a thing like that.

We went about our business the rest of the day cleaning the cabin and doing other chores. After I got my chores done, I decided to go fishing. I asked if anyone else wanted to go, but everybody else was too busy, so I went alone. I usually didn't have to go that far to put my pole in the water to get beautiful rainbow trout, but this year the river went underground in front of the cabin, so I had to go looking for the river. As I was walking along the dry riverbed to find it, I saw another strange thing: a headless fish. It looked like the head was bitten off. I'd never run across anything like this before. To say I was uneasy was an understatement, but there had to be some explanation for all this. I wasn't really afraid yet, because, after all, I was at home in the wilderness. I also noticed the absence of wildlife. Not even the deer were coming out to lick the salt blocks Gary left in the field near the cabin like he did the years before. That was very unusual, since every time before this, there were all kinds of deer in the area.

As I was walking toward the river and away from the cabins, I heard a commotion in the thicket. It startled me at first. It was a young deer. It was the only deer I saw on the whole trip, lying down hiding herself. It suddenly jumped up and ran away. She scared me almost as much as I scared her, since I was on edge anyway. I was walking down the dry riverbed till I started hearing a trickle of water, and as I kept walking, I heard more water, and then all of a sudden there was a rushing river. It was very strange, but once there, I spent a while fishing till I caught four or five nice rainbow trout. Then I took them back to the cabin and made a fire. After cleaning them, I fried them in the skillet for each of us. We also brought some potatoes, and after Renae cut them up, we fried them up with the fish and had a nice dinner. After eating, we sat around the fire, and I told them about what I had just gone through on my little fishing trip. Then we roasted marshmallows and made our favorite dessert, s'mores. After that, we decided to turn in before anything else unexpected happened, but I noticed it was still unusually quiet.

The next day, we planned an all-day bike ride into the foothills of the mountain range. We woke up early and couldn't wait to get at what we enjoyed most, exploring and motorcycle riding. Larry drove the pickup so if anything happened to one of the bikes, it could be hauled back to the cabin, especially since we were traveling quite some distances along logging trails and dirt roads.

The day started out pretty well and was exhilarating. The only incident we had was Renae falling off the bike and burning her leg on the tailpipe, which was extremely painful, I'm sure. Except for the burn, which was going to leave a nasty scar, she was okay. Nearing the end of the day, we decided to turn back toward the cabin while it was still daylight.

As I was riding behind Gary on the back of his bike, I noticed we lost a black leather bag with a camera and medical supplies in it, so we stopped to look for it. Larry went on ahead to the cabin in the pickup. We never could find the bag. The sun was nearing the horizon, so we decided we had to get back as soon as possible. Larry was at the cabin alone, and it seemed like everything unusual happened at dusk, so we had to make it back because it was getting dark quickly.

As we walked into the house, Larry was sitting on the couch waiting for us with an ax in his hands, as if he was protecting himself. We couldn't help but notice the look on his face. He was white as a ghost, and his hands were shaking as he tried to explain what happened to him. He said, "While I was driving down the driveway to the cabin, a large hairy creature came out of the woods and hit the front of the pickup. He was so tall his upper body bent over the hood, and as he straightened up, he stared right into my eyes. Then he turned around and ran away, swinging his arms and taking huge strides, and then disappeared back into the woods."

After listening to Larry tell us this story, I was definitely afraid; but after that long trip on the bike, I had to go to the outhouse.

Unfortunately, it was around the log cabin, then to the other side of the field at the edge of the woods; and it was getting dark. So I decided to go right behind the big empty log cabin. While I was there, I felt an uneasy presence. As I was pulling my pants down, I heard a growl behind me. It couldn't have been a bear. I know what a bear sounds like because they have a kind of hollow sound to their growl. This was more like a dog or even a human. He growled twice. "Grrrr, grrrr." I was hoping it was Larry playing a trick on me because, as he was talking before about his ordeal with the monster, I thought he might have been telling us a story. I wasn't really sure I believed him, but as I turned to go back, I looked up above me into the glassless window of the cabin and saw a hairy face with angry eyes glaring down at me and his teeth clenched as he growled. I quickly pulled my pants up, and within seconds, still breathless from running faster than I'd ever run before, I found myself back at the smaller cabin. Renae and her brothers were just outside taking things out of the pickup and putting them away. They could see that I was pretty shaken up as I explained what I saw, so we decided to pack up everything and leave for home the next morning. I was so scared I couldn't sleep. If we could have left that night, I'm sure we would have, but it was safer to leave in the daylight. The next morning when I went to the outhouse, Renae went with me. Then we packed up and left for home.

Since that time, I have seen documentaries on television and read some articles on sightings of this elusive creature, the Sasquatch or Bigfoot. It was said in one documentary that in order to claim their territory for mating or whatever reason, they leave signs in their area. This time, I believe the signs were the headless pheasant and fish to scare off any invaders like us.

One article said that the Sasquatch doesn't mean any harm to humans. They're just trying to live as reclusive a life as possible so as not to come in contact with humans, but industrialization and logging are probably causing the near extinction of this beast who could possibly be part human, part animal. Since they are intelligent, and not seen by most humans, very few people believe he exists. I've seen, so therefore, I believe. So far I've seen one president, the queen of England, and now a Sasquatch in my life.

21

CHAPTER 3

MEETING MY FIRST HUSBAND

I always wanted to be like my eldest brother, Gary. He was a fireman for the San Diego Fire Department, but he drank constantly when he was off duty. He liked beer, so I liked beer too. He even bought me a bottle of champagne for my graduation present, and I drank the whole thing myself. I got real sick as he and my future first husband we're driving around with me in the back seat. Unfortunately, I don't remember much of my graduation. I also had an aunt (my mother's sister) and uncle who drank a lot of beer; and when I went to visit them, while they were camping in Oregon, they allowed me to drink all I wanted. I was only sixteen, but that made me feel grown up, so I never really overdid it like blacking out or making a fool of myself. On the other hand, my dad, even though he was in the Navy, did not drink, because when he was born on the Crow Indian Reservation in Montana, he saw what alcohol did to the Indians; and because of that, he never drank, as far as I knew. He didn't even allow it in the house.

During my teenage years, I had a lot of boyfriends, but I was very particular. I made sure they were gentlemen who let me drink but never took advantage of me sexually when I drank. I would go out with them on Friday night and drink so much that I would black out and be sick and crawl up the stairs when I got home. The next morning on Saturday, at nine o'clock, I had to wake up and go bowling, most of the time with a hangover. I still maintained a 172 average. At seventeen, I started going out with a guy named John, a few years older than me, who didn't drink or do drugs. He not only knew Jimi Hendrix but was also his best friend when he was alive. He showed me pictures of them together. One day, a new guy, named Andy, came in and joined my bowling league. He said he was seventeen going on eighteen, but he was actually twenty going on twenty-one, which I didn't find out till way later. He lied about his age because he wanted to bowl on my team, and officially after he turned twenty-one, he was too old to bowl in the junior league. At that time, I was going with John. He was a nice guy, but I really didn't have any feelings for him. Then one day, Andy came over to the house, while John was there; and I noticed Andy shaved off his scraggly beard. Suddenly, he looked so handsome, and I immediately had an attraction to Andy, so I dropped John like a rock. Unfortunately, after I got to know Andy better, he introduced me to pot and other drugs. Before I started drinking, at age thirteen, I swore I'd never be like the other girls in school and do drugs and get pregnant; but because of Andy, I ended up doing both. I shouldn't really blame him because if it wasn't him, it probably would have been someone else.

My senior year was very tumultuous because in 1971, they started bussing the blacks in from the central area; and because they also eliminated the middle schools, they added 1,500 new students that year. Because of it, we had three riots and two bombings. I felt like we were in a war zone. One day, they had a riot in the lunch room, where my friend Pam and the principal were hit in the head with stools. I was in math class right above the lunch room, and it felt like an earthquake beneath us. We had to evacuate the school, and as I was walking home, I noticed down the street two black girls looking through a white girl's purse, so I went the other way and ran home as fast as I could. My parents weren't the type I could go to and talk about anything, especially what was going on at school, so I held all my fears inside me. I felt I needed to drink and do drugs to cope with what was going on in my life at the time. So to me, Andy was helping me to cope. I promised myself I would never be prejudiced against blacks or African Americans, even after that, because it wasn't their fault they had to be bussed across town to our school.

While I was going with Andy, I got pregnant; and when I turned eighteen, I had an abortion. My parents never found out. Afterward, my parents gave me a one-way ticket to Michigan for my graduation present. That's where my elder sister, Bonnie, lived. My sister went to church and was a Christian, and in a way, I thought this escape to Michigan would be a cure for my alcohol and drug problems. After I got there, Andy sold his bicycle and came out to Michigan, where we got baptized and joined the church and then got married. I felt like it was a new life and things would be wonderful, but the devil had other plans. Soon, not understanding the mind of an alcoholic and addict, we were tempted again when we went bowling. We started doing drugs again. Needless to say, excuses started popping up, and we stopped going to church even though it was only four houses down the block. Then I had a miscarriage, and right after recovering from that, we lost the house we were renting. We decided to live with a family whose mother was mentally ill, but we knew the kids did drugs, and we thought that was great. We ended up living in the basement and sleeping on a mattress on the floor. The window was broken, so a cat kept coming in, and because of that, we had lice all over us. I finally got so distraught I decided to stop doing drugs and go back to church and change my life again. God heard my cry, and soon we were able to buy a new house in a low-income subdivision a few miles away in another town. After we got married, Andy got a job working for the Village of Caro in the water department and had the company truck, so the first vehicle we bought in Michigan was a 500 Kawasaki motorcycle. It was considered the quickest bike on the road. I actually got it up to 110 miles per hour, thanks to Michigan's long straight country roads. When I was sixteen, in Seattle, the first vehicle I ever bought was a 250 Honda, which I painted purple and had a stars-and-stripes helmet. I wore a tie-dyed shirt, so I looked like the typical hippy back then.

We bought a brand-new house and moved from Caro to a smaller town in the middle of the farmland called Fairgrove. Andy got a construction job and worked around the state of Michigan and Chicago and was gone all the time. He was making a lot of money, but I was very lonely living there. I bought a dirt bike, a 175 Yamaha

Enduro, and rode motocross racing while Andy was gone. I never won any races, but it was fun and kept me busy while he was gone. Sometimes he would leave me a ten-dollar bill and not come home for two weeks. Thank goodness I didn't need a lot of money to fill the gas tank. When I ran out of food, I'd go over to the church elder's house and eat with them. Later, I also bought a 500 Yamaha motorcycle. One time we both rode our bikes to Cedar Point in Sandusky, Ohio. He rode the 500 Kawasaki. When we got near the amusement park, it was getting dark, so we slept in a cornfield and woke up the next day and spent all day on the rides, then we went to the same cornfield, slept overnight, and rode home the next day. Who needs a motel when you're young and not picky?

Then I got a job working at a plastics factory in Millington, Michigan, which was about fifty miles away from where we lived. Before I got this job, we bought a little 1967 Spitfire convertible. We found it in a garage full of leaves. It belonged to a lady whose husband died, so we got it pretty cheap. All it needed was a tune-up to get it started. Since it was great on gas and my job was so far away, I would drive it to work, and it was getting too cold to ride the motorcycle. It was during the winter months when Andy was laid off from work. This happened to become the worst weather condition in Michigan history, and I happened to be working the midnight shift: 11:00 p.m. to 7:00 a.m. I liked working that time shift because I could get a lot of things done during the day, but sometimes I would forget to sleep, and one time I was up for thirty-six hours and fell asleep on the way home from work and found myself driving on the side of the road. I made sure I got some sleep after that. Then the blizzards came. One night, the snow was so bad I couldn't see, but Andy said we needed the money, and he made me go anyway. It was the wind that blew me off the road across traffic into a gully. Andy got mad at me for hurting the car because I bent an axial. He didn't seem to care if I was injured, because my head hit the back of the seat, which was metal; and I blacked out for a few minutes. He was just concerned about the car. Then another time, the heater in the car didn't work, and on the way home, the temperature was 60 below zero, windchill factor, and the convertible top was flapping in the wind. By the time I got home, my feet and hands were almost frostbitten. I had to warm up in the bathtub.

I only liked that job because I made some incredible friends: two girls who were best friends, almost like sisters, and were my supervisors. It was springtime, and one of them started going to church and said she got baptized and saved. Then one night, while we were in the break room, the one going to church told me and the other girl about a dream she had. She said that her friend died; and while she was crying, the friend called out to her and said, "Don't cry, because I'm all right."

Then she said, "Oh, you're not dead?"

Her friend said to her, "Oh yes, I'm in heaven with Jesus." I thought that was a weird dream, but her friend didn't think it was weird at all, which I thought was strange. Two days later, there was a horrific accident. That friend the dream was about was on the back of her boyfriend's motorcycle when they ran into a semitruck. It was raining, and the roads were slick. The cars stopped suddenly in front of them. When he tried to avoid them, he went into oncoming traffic, hitting the semi's tires; but while she was in the middle of the road, two cars going around the accident ran over her. Her boyfriend survived to tell me about it when I went to the hospital to visit. The weirdest part was what he told me next. He said, "Right before she got on the bike, she said she wouldn't mind if her life ended that night because she found the Lord and her life was complete."

I think I was affected more than her best friend. I quit the job right after that and just stayed home. Andy was working again, so I was alone. I didn't know it, but I went into a deep depression. I just felt numb. Then one day, as I was vacuuming the house, I looked into the mirror; and I had little red spots all over my face. They were all over my body too. I called my friends in the church, and they told me to go to the ER. The doctor took blood tests and put me in isolation immediately. I couldn't get visitors except looking through the windows. Andy came home from work to visit me and had to wear a mask and gown to enter the room. They couldn't figure out what I had, but my white blood cells were so low they thought I had leukemia. Then when I started getting all the attention with people looking through the windows and the glass doors at me, I started getting better, and my blood count started going up. That's where I learned that you can die from depression, and I couldn't handle death.

At twenty-one years old, I had a little girl named Sunny. Later, when Andy would get laid off, we would travel around the country, first in a Volkswagen van and later in a motor home. Once, when Jennifer was only six weeks old, we left for California; and when we got home, she was six months old. That was the year we went by way of Washington State to visit my best friend, Renae, then down the coast to visit his brother in San Diego. Then another year, we drove to Key West, Florida, to visit my parents and spent six weeks there. Later on, we bought a four-wheel-drive motor home, and on the way back from Washington State, we drove through Colorado and planned to snow ski in Aspen, but as we were driving during the night, we went through a blizzard. That's what we bought the four-wheel drive for. We had a long line of vehicles following us because the visibility was horrible, so we had to stop at Copper Mountain, instead of Aspen. We happened to park right next to a nice hotel. The next day, we took turns skiing and watching the baby. The hotel had a spa with a swimming pool that had a glass overhead that kept you warm when you swam under it. And the pool went outside. It was neat to watch the steam rising from the water as it was nice and warm and the air freezing. Because of the blizzard the night before, the skiing was phenomenal. As I was skiing, I looked down, and I was knee deep in wonderful fluffy powder. I'm used to skiing in the Pacific Northwest where the skiing is mediocre at best. Icy most of the time. Very much a challenge especially as you're learning. Growing up, I never really thought I could ski that well until we got here. After skiing, we would go in to the lodge and sit by the huge fireplace and act like one of the guests. The only expense was our food and lift tickets.

Whenever we got to California, at Andy's brother's house, I was always very lonely because the two of them would go out together and leave me at his house alone with the baby every evening. They couldn't care less about me. That's why I was lonely all the time. When we got home, and Andy started working again, I went through the summer months alone and bored, taking care of the baby, and not able to get away and ride the motorcycle like before. I kept going over to the elders' house, but I could tell they were getting tired of me. Then as Andy was on the other side of the state, I decided to go to the store and get a bottle of wine. I drank it and went to bed with no real consequences. So a week later, I went to the store and decided to get two bottles of wine. After drinking that, in a blackout, I must have called somebody at church; and they called my brother to come over and see if I was okay. They came over and found me throwing up on my back. I could have died like Jimi Hendrix, but they found me in time.

My brother's new wife, Amanda, had a father who was in Alcoholics Anonymous; and she took me to my first AA meeting. When I went with her, all who were there were older men. Needless to say, I couldn't relate to anything that they had to tell me because I was different. I was a young female, only twenty-two years old. I couldn't be an alcoholic. So two weeks later, after my husband got laid off for the winter, I joined a bowling league. While he was watching the baby, I went to bowl. As I was bowling, I had seven screwdrivers. On the way home, I stopped at the nearest store and got a bottle of wine. Then I drove past our town to the next town and went to the nearest bar. I went inside and sat at the bar next to this creepy-looking guy. He proceeded to tell me he had some good pot at his house, and I said, "Okay, let's go get it." He then asked me if I had a car to drive because he was on his motorcycle, and I said I had a Volkswagen van outside. It was a camper van we used to go around the country in. We went outside to get into the van, and he said, "Let's get in the back of the van and let my friend drive."

I said, "Okay," especially since I was pretty drunk already. When we got there, all I remember was taking a drink, and then I woke up on my back in a bedroom with this guy on top of me. When I tried to get up and get away, I saw a fist coming down on the side of my head. Then I woke up in the back of my van at a gas station. As I was sitting up and getting my bearings, I looked around and saw a bunch of guys getting out of the van, yelling, "It's on fire! Let's run!" All I could think about was getting away from those guys. I noticed the flames behind me, but I realized I was half naked, so as quickly as I could, I found some clothing and put it on. I then made my way to the front of the van to try to start it. I then realized the engine in the back was on fire, and flames were coming out and getting closer, so I jumped out of the van and stood there and watched it burn to the ground next to the gas pumps. I was right across the street from the fire department, but it was a volunteer fire department, and they didn't get there until the van was completely engulfed and burned down to the tires. If I hadn't woken up, they would have left me in the van to burn. One of the firemen took me home, and my husband consoled me at first, and then he started yelling at me and telling me what a whore I was to go out and do that to myself.

The next morning, I woke up with the most severe headache I've ever had in my life. I felt like I had a concussion and my head was going to explode. I even had a black-and-blue ring behind my ear where that fist came down on my head. Andy then took me to the doctor to have me checked to see if I had a concussion and if I was raped. It was more than embarrassing. It was humiliating to the extent I wanted to die. That afternoon, we went to one of the church deacons' house for dinner. I couldn't eat a thing. I was still in shock and feeling very numb. I just sat there and took my fork and played with my food until everyone was done. I looked up and noticed everyone was just sitting there staring at me. Then they took turns, one by one, starting with my brother, yelling at me, saying how much I hated myself for doing what I did, especially with a baby at home. They called that "tough love." I just wanted to crawl into a hole and die. One day, I was very depressed, and while driving down the road, I felt like someone hugging me, and I heard a voice say to me out loud, "Nancy, I still love you."

After that, I started going to see a counselor who was an ex-drug addict. It seemed to be exactly what I needed at the time. He empathized with what I was going through: my loneliness and postpartum depression. He even blamed my husband for leaving me at home alone a lot and the church for not helping me when I needed it, by ignoring my calls for help. They never came to visit me. He got me to realize how much better a person I was and made me feel like life was worth living. After a year, I went out and got a real estate license.

Someone at church even told me to not worry if I couldn't pass the test because this other lady couldn't pass the test and she had a college degree. I took the test and passed it the first time. Everyone was shocked. I figured they thought I was not very intelligent because of my alcohol problem. I sold real estate for two years, and I even made enough money to buy a 1971 Pontiac GTO. I was starting to get happy and doing well when Andy wanted me move to Lansing. He was working there and in Chicago. I didn't want to go, but he threatened to take away our daughter and give her to my sister if I didn't move with him. So we moved and lived in our motor home in a trailer park just outside of Lansing. Soon after, I picked up a six-pack and started drinking again.

Chapter 4

Meeting Ollie

Then I got a job at Denny's working midnights so my husband could watch the baby while I worked. I was so fed up and wanted to leave him that I was looking for another place to live. I even asked one of the other waitresses if she had a room at her place for me and my daughter. But then I met Ollie. He and his friend would come in to Denny's and eat after work every night. He told me he was the manager of a bowling alley, and I told him I used to bowl as a junior bowler, so he invited me to come over and bowl. When he saw me bowl, he asked me if I wanted to work for him as his secretary, and of course I said yes. I wasn't attracted to him at first because of his age. He was in his forties. I was just twenty-four; but by the way he cared for me, with what I was going through, I soon fell in love with him. He told me that he and his wife weren't in love anymore and were going to separate. I was married to my husband for six years by that time. Because Ollie was twenty years older, some people objected to our getting together and said it would never last, especially his eldest daughter. Not long after that, Ollie and I both lost our jobs because when the owner met my husband, Andy, he hired him at the lanes too. He thought Andy looked so clean cut, he tried to split Ollie and me up by sending me to the other lanes as an assistant manager, but that didn't work, so we moved in together.

Soon after we moved in together, Ollie's wife went out and got a job at a hospital. A few days later, she was walking across the street to her job, and a car hit and killed her. We were taking care of their son, J.R., at the time; and I had to be the one to tell him. It was devastating for him. I felt very guilty. I was glad that she and I got together before she died. After that, Ollie and I lived together for three years.

We moved into an apartment and got jobs as janitors at another bowling lanes with a professional grade golf course. It was during the summer, so I learned to golf. I also started adding peppermint schnapps to my coffee in the morning. When we got home from work, I would walk over to the convenient store, right next to the apartments we lived in, and buy a quart of beer. It soon turned into more than one quart a night. One day at work, I discovered the bar in the back that was closed for the summer. The beer taps were free flowing, if you know what I mean. I was drinking from morning till night. My alcohol tolerance level must have been escalating quite a bit because no one noticed I was drunk all day. Even Ollie thought I just had a hangover from the quarts of beer the night before. Needless to say, after a couple of months, we lost that job as well. Ollie then got hired as a manager at another smaller bowling lanes on the other side of town, and because we had no money, we had to move out of our apartment, but thank goodness, there happened to be a one-room block house right behind the bowling alley. They were using it for storage, so we cleaned it up, as best we could, and moved in. I figured there wasn't enough room for Sunny, so I took her to my sister's house up in Caro, about one hundred miles away. I knew I couldn't take care of her with the way I was drinking anyway. Every morning I would go into the bowling alley and turn on a lane and bowl for about two hours, which added up to about thirty games of bowling. Then I would go into the bar and John, the bartender, who liked me, would have a draft beer waiting for me. I proceeded to drink until I either blacked out or passed out and Ollie would carry me home to that little block house. Soon I was sick of the way I was living and hit a bottom. (One of many in my alcoholic career). I decided to start divorce proceedings, which the court made us wait six months for it to be final. So I moved up to my sister's house to clean up my act; since my sister, being a good Christian woman, was very much against alcohol, I couldn't drink, and I could be with Sunny. It was exactly what I needed at the time. I went through some withdrawals and even threw up, but my sister just thought I had low blood sugar.

CHAPTER 5

JOINING THE NAVY

Soon I started getting a lot of energy back and was working out and even running about three miles a day. One morning I went into town and walked by a Navy recruiter's office and signed up. I was twenty-six at the time and the cutoff was twenty-six, but I had to wait six months, delayed enlistment, which would make me twenty-seven at the time of going to boot camp, so I had signed a waiver, which was fine with me. They just wanted to make their quota. After some tests, they told me I had skills for mechanics and they were trying to get more females in the hull technician rate. They told me I would be one of the first females on ships. I thought that was so cool and exciting. I made arrangements for Bonnie to take care of Sunny for the first year or until the end of her school year. I planned to marry Ollie and he would later bring her to me and we would be a family again. Six months later, I went to Lansing to finalize my divorce. The next week, on August 1st, 1982, Ollie and I got married on the lawn of his eldest daughter's apartment. The next day, I went to Detroit to the recruitment headquarters to fly out to boot camp in Orlando, Florida. Not much of a honeymoon, but my plans came true.

What a time to join. It was August and ninety degrees in the shade, but I was full of energy. My body was pretty much detoxed after six months of not drinking, and I was ready for anything. I needed a new start on life, and this was it. I was twenty-seven years old and the oldest one there. I even had to have a waiver for my age when I joined, so a lot of the girls looked up to me for help, especially with folding clothes and shining boots. I was a natural at domestic things like making beds and shining boots thanks to my mother, but I was very good in sports and exercises, like push-ups and running. I even won a contest doing pull-ups, and my company commanders loved me for that. Somebody told me never to volunteer in the Navy, but when they asked us to stand up and sing a solo if we wanted to be in the choir, I jumped at the chance since I liked singing at church. That got me out of a lot of extra work, and I loved every minute of it.

On the last day of boot camp, my parents came for the graduation ceremony and took me out to dinner. They were so proud of me, and we went out and had pizza. But all I could see around me were people drinking beer, and that's all I could think about. So after they dropped me off on the base, I was walking toward the barracks and noticed the Enlisted Club. I walked in and started drinking, and after that, I vaguely remember standing in the entrance to the barracks with my hat on backward and saluting inside, which is not allowed in the Navy. Then I woke up the next morning, thinking like I usually did when I blacked out, *I'm in my rack and safe*, while the other girls were mad at me for some reason. Probably because they had to carry me in, but I've never found out exactly why. Whatever it was, I definitely made a fool out of myself.

CHAPTER 6

GRADUATION AND A SCHOOL

I graduated as an E3 because I attended Lansing Community College one year for business management. Then I was off to HT A School, where I was to learn my trade as a welder, plumber, sheet metal worker, and firefighter. Also, with damage control, I had to learn to keep the ship afloat when disaster strikes. My job also included nuclear, biological, and chemical warfare, which was highly classified at the time since it was during the Cold War period. This was a time in 1982 when they were trying to fill this rate with women, since it was traditionally a male rate, and women were being introduced to ships. I took some tests in the recruiters' station before I joined that showed I was mechanically inclined. Therefore, I qualified to be a hull technician or HT. Since I was quite a tomboy, anyway, why not? We women were actually pioneers in our field.

I was sent to HT A School at the Philadelphia naval base. And since it was near the docks, it was dirty and grungy, and it was the beginning of fall, so it was cold and rainy. Our living quarters looked like the projects: dilapidated two-story old apartments. We had to muster (as the Navy calls it) every morning and evening in front of the two buildings, the left side for men and the right side for women. The women faced the men and had to be counted. The men, or boys, as I saw them, let us know that we, as women, were not welcome. One guy even hung his body parts outside the window, yelling, "You cunts don't belong in our Navy." I tried to be tough and not to let it bother me, but it really made me feel sick inside. As a good comeback, one girl yelled, "Get the tweezers!"

We, as students, had to meet at a place to be picked up every morning by big trucks pulling, what they called, cattle cars. They were used to haul cattle in before but modified them by putting poles inside to hold on to as we were crowded in and were standing up. Kind of like buses. All I could think about was this was just a temporary situation so I could get through it even though it felt very intimidating and scary at the time. My fear of being raped kept me from drinking for the first two weeks, and it was a real fear because at least two girls came to me and told me they had been raped after they got there. I was the elder, so they would confide in me, but there was no one for me to confide in since there were only men in charge above me, so I never told anyone to this day. I also remembered the incident I had with my first husband when I was beaten and raped and left in the van to burn. I figured I learned from that experience.

Then I discovered the Enlisted Club. I made some friends so that if I drank, I wouldn't be alone. That was my only defense against getting raped. My drinking after class escalated to the point I started having blackouts where all I remembered was putting down the glass on the side of the pool table and walking out the door. I woke up the next morning in my rack, relieved that I made it back to the barracks safe. I found out that the way I protected myself, someone told me, that they saw me playing pool at the club, put down my glass, and after walking to the door, I would start running as fast as I could to the barracks, so they tackled me, and I just kept saying, "I have to run so I don't get raped." They didn't understand, but I knew what I was doing even though it was subconscious and in a blackout.

One day, I came in to class with a serious hangover. I must have looked pretty bad, and I felt just like I looked. I didn't realize it at the time, but some of the chiefs teaching the classes were in the program of Alcoholics Anonymous, and they were watching me every day. That day, my chief instructor came up to me and asked me if I might have a problem with alcohol, and I said, "Yes, maybe." Well, that was all they needed, because off to the doctor I went to be evaluated. He said, "You are a chronic alcoholic, and you need to go to rehab

ASAP." Those words cut me like a knife. I had never been called an alcoholic before. Well, they immediately put me on Antabuse, and I had to go back to the school and wait for them to process the paperwork for rehab. While I was in a booth learning how to weld, I couldn't control my hands because they were shaking so much, and I was zapping everything. I didn't realize I was going through the DTS or delirium tremors, which can cause shakes and hallucinations. I suddenly ran out of the booth and to the corpsman's office in sick bay. I looked at her and started laughing and then started crying at the same time. She was looking in the medical book and said, "I didn't think Antabuse did this to you." She had no idea I was going through alcohol withdrawal.

CHAPTER 7
OFF TO REHAB

Before I left for the rehab, there was a young man who said he would pray for me. He invited me to a prayer meeting out in the yard, and they all said a prayer for me. I believe to this day he was an angel sent by God to give me comfort. I never saw him again. A few days later, I boarded a small medivac plane and took off on my way to rehab, which was in Great Lakes, Illinois. I told them my family was in Michigan, and if I didn't get to a rehab near them, I would kill myself. Thank goodness they took me seriously and sent me to the nearest rehab on a naval base in Great Lakes, near Michigan. I was thinking of my daughter, Sunny, at the time and how much I missed her and how I could be there during Christmas; so I was already figuring out a way to see her.

During the flight, I became very ill with bronchitis. I figured we would be in Great Lakes later on that day; but I had no idea, being on a medivac plane, we would be flying up and down the East Coast, stopping at different hospitals on the way to our destination, taking us a full week to get there. At the end of the first day, they decided to stay overnight at McGuire Air Force Base, where we parked right next to Air Force One, the president's plane, which was an awesome sight; and I stayed overnight in Bethesda Naval Hospital. The next time, we stayed a few nights in a hospital in Illinois. By that time, I was pretty sick and on medication for my lungs, which was making me very sleepy.

When I first got there, I saw a lot of commotion going on, then a man with his little baby in his arms sat next to me in the waiting room. He told me they just had a tornado touch down in his mobile home park and found his one-year-old daughter a half mile away without a scratch on her. "What a miracle," I told him. Later, they were bringing more people in because of a flood. They finally found a bed for me in a room with a couple of other people. I was just glad to lie down even though sitting up was easier to breathe, being sick and all.

The next day around lunchtime, I was trying to sleep; and when I opened my eyes, I was nose to nose with a German shepherd. I found out later someone called in a bomb threat somewhere in the hospital. So in the three days I was there, I went through a tornado, a flood, and a bomb scare. That's enough to handle in a lifetime let alone in three days and in one hospital.

CHAPTER 8
GETTING TO REHAB

I finally made it to the alcohol rehab center; and I started to feel a lot better, from the bronchitis, that is. Mentally and emotionally, I was full of fear and apprehension and wondering what was going to happen to me. I had one female roommate named Amy. We were the only two females in the whole rehab. My fear was overwhelming, and I covered my feelings with anger, especially toward men. I know now that my feelings and emotions were because of detoxing from alcohol. I look back on it and feel very sorry for the young man who happened to get in my way, and because of my thoughts of paranoia, I threw a cup of coffee on him. For some reason, I thought he was going to attack me. Of course he wasn't. I walked around with my fists clenched in front of me as if I was trying to protect myself. From what, I don't know. All during counseling sessions, I kept thinking of beating up the counselor on my way out the door just because he said he was an atheist. I thought I knew all about God because I was taught the Bible in church, but my thoughts of God were so distorted, all I wanted to do was kill or hurt people. I was so full of hatred, especially toward myself because of what I had become, an alcoholic and a horrible mother. I never thought of suicide, but I felt I didn't deserve to live.

Somehow, being in rehab gave me a sense of hope. This hope kept me going and wanting to live. As the days went by, I started feeling better and getting more energy. Three weeks went by, and soon it was Christmastime. I wanted to go and see my daughter and my new husband, Ollie. They almost didn't let me go, but I begged them to, and they did, reluctantly. I only got three days' leave, so my husband came down to get me, and we went back and spent the night in Lansing. The next day, we went up to see my daughter in Caro, Michigan, about a hundred miles northeast of there. I could only go in and see her for a few minutes as it was nighttime, and she was sleeping. My sister objected, but I woke Sunny up and told her I loved her. We both held each other and cried, but I told her I had to go back to work. I knew she didn't understand, but I was still glad I got to see her and hold her even if it was for just a moment. Time was short, so we had to leave right then and there so we could make it back by the next day.

I managed to get through the next three weeks of rehab without incident. The day before graduation, they put me and Amy on a stage while they, the counselors, evaluated us in front of everyone else. They said, "Amy tried to commit suicide twice and got into a serious car accident and almost died, but we think she'll get sober and make it. Nancy, on the other hand, we think she'll die drunk." I guess I must not have made a very good impression while I was there. I was pretty insane. People tell me it was their way of making me try harder. Either way, I felt I needed more time, but six weeks was all they allowed me. Still full of fear, I didn't think I was ready, but I was sent back to Philadelphia A School anyway. One thing I did get out of it was a desire to stop drinking, and in Alcoholics Anonymous, that's a beginning.

CHAPTER 9

GRADUATION AND MY FIRST DUTY STATION

This was a time when alcohol rehabs were fairly new in the Navy, and they had no real aftercare program, so I had to create my own. I instructed them to put me on Antabuse, and I also told them that I needed a duty driver to take me to AA meetings after school. It was pretty strange, telling them what to do, but I got my way, and because of it, I finished fifth in my class. As a result, I was given a choice of where I wanted go on my first tour of duty; so I asked for a duty station as far south on the East Coast as possible to be near my parents, who were in Florida. I got Mayport, Florida, just north of Jacksonville.

I was sent to a SIMA, which stands for Shore Intermediate Maintenance Activity. Basically, we repaired the ships that were stationed there, mostly destroyers.

I started working in the pipe shop, but that only lasted a week. As soon as I checked in, they asked me if I wanted to go out drinking, but I told them, "No! I just got out of alcohol rehab." Their answer to me was "So what? We've been in several rehabs, and now we know how to drink even better." Totally opposite of the chiefs in A school. I noticed most of them rode motorcycles too. They seemed just like a motorcycle gang in uniform. For the first week, the chief and crew would not let me go back to my barracks to sleep at night until I played cards with them, so I slept on the desk. I finally decided to start playing poker with them and won a lot of money. Then they changed the game to dice, and I lost all my winnings plus $110. So I snuck off back to the barracks without permission and stayed there till they came looking for me a couple of days later. I was afraid they were going to put me on charges of AWOL (absence without leave). They came by and told me they wanted me to go out drinking with them.

When I came back to work on Monday morning, they said I was transferred to the sheet metal shop. I knew it was because they were afraid I would tell the captain about the gambling. I never said a thing. I was just glad to get out of that situation, and the sheet metal shop was a lot cleaner and better environment too. I noticed that the guys accepted me as a fellow sailor and not just another female to harass. The chief treated me pretty good also. I loved learning how to weld on aluminum and using the giant machinery and equipment every day. I worked with a few young men (I was the only female), designing and building salad bars and sneeze shields for all the destroyers in Mayport, plus other jobs that were needed. When I would give advice to the guys who even had more experience than me, they would listen and say, "You've got some good ideas." I was surprised that a man would listen to me because my self-esteem was so low. Probably from the way my first husband treated me.

One day, while we were working in the shop, we heard a lot of commotion going on just outside the door, so we went out to look, and there was a missile lying on the pier pointed right at us. Someone on the ship had pushed the wrong button and sent a missile off in our direction. Fortunately, it wasn't armed, but it was scary. It still could have caused a lot of damage and maybe even hurt or killed us if it had hit the building we were in.

Another day we were working up on the mast of a ship. It was pretty high up, and thank goodness I wasn't afraid of heights. In fact, when I was younger, around two or three years old, I used to climb up the basketball pole and swing on the basket like a monkey, so I was pretty good at jobs like this one, but the guy that I was working with wasn't. At that time, we weren't wearing any safety harnesses. All of a sudden, he lost his grip and started to fall. I grabbed his belt and held him until he got his grip again. Needless to say, he was grateful I was there close to him and had very good reflexes. Me too.

At the end of the school year in Michigan, Ollie was bringing Sunny down so we could be a family, but we had nowhere to live and not enough money saved up. My parents gave me $500 to get either a car or a place to live, but instead, I went out and got drunk with a work friend, and before we went out, I gave him the money so I wouldn't lose it. When we got back to the barracks, he said he gave me back the money and I put it in my wallet and in my pants pocket. Then, before I went up to my room, I went to the bathroom downstairs, which was a big mistake, because the wallet must have fallen out of my pocket. When I woke up the next morning, I noticed my wallet missing. I went downstairs and asked the petty officer on watch if he found a wallet, and he said yes and gave it to me. When I looked in it, of course it was empty. I asked him if there was any money in it, and he said, "No, it was empty when I found it." And then he said, "I guess someone must have taken it," looking like a Cheshire cat; but there was nothing I could do about it. I knew I was the guilty one, and I deserved to lose the money because I was the one who chose to go out and drink. Because of that, I had to find a motel for us to stay in and borrow money from my friend whom I went out drinking with. I felt humiliated but unfortunately not enough to stop drinking. Maybe for just a short time. I found out that with an alcoholic, it's not stopping because I could stop anytime I wanted to; it's not being able to stay stopped that makes a person an alcoholic.

After Sunny got out of school for the year, Ollie picked her and Tasha (the cat) up from my sister's house in Caro and finally started their way down to Florida. They were driving an old Ford Pinto wagon, and while going through Atlanta, Georgia, the engine blew up, and they were stuck there in one-hundred-degree heat until I could go get them. Thank goodness I found a fellow sailor in another shop who was willing to help me and had a pickup truck. His name was Joe, and he was a very large Native American.

On the way up, it was my turn to drive, and he kept telling me to go faster so we could get back to work the next day, so I was going about ninety miles an hour when a cop stopped us. The sailor whom I asked to help was tall and had a pretty big head, and he looked kind of intimidating, especially from the back. When I stopped on the side of the freeway, I saw the cop had his gun out from the back of the truck, pointing it toward us. He was yelling, "Get out of the truck, now!" but we just looked at each other and stayed there, afraid to move. After all, this was Georgia. He yelled at us again, "Get out of the truck!" When he came up to us, gun in his hand, he saw me and Joe and asked, "Why are you going so fast?" We told him the situation with my husband and daughter, breaking down in the middle of Atlanta, and that we were in the military, stationed in Mayport. We also told him we were in a hurry because we had to be back to work the next day. He turned out to be a nice guy and decided not to give us a ticket and told us to keep our speed down to seventy-five to eighty and we wouldn't get stopped.

When we got back, I found a motel, but we still had no vehicle. I was going to a few AA meetings, and a friend in AA offered us a room to live in at his house. I jumped at it. It was a bedroom with only a mattress on the floor, but it was cheaper than a motel and close to the base. Unfortunately, we had no privacy whatsoever.

CHAPTER 10

BOWLING FOR THE NAVY

I got into my first bowling tournament representing the Navy, the Southeast Regionals, including Puerto Rico and the US Virgin Islands. I won first place, which put my foot in the door for the All-Navy team. I was thankfully blessed with a captain who liked sports.

Then came the tryouts for the All-Navy Team. For that, I needed a letter of recommendation from a professional bowler; and just before I left Lansing, Michigan, I got to know Joe Joseph who is in the Professional Bowlers Hall of Fame. He, very graciously, sent my captain a letter of recommendation, who was also impressed with me for winning the Southeast Regionals. I was soon on my way to Corpus Christi, Texas, on the Navy base, to try out for the All-Navy Team. I bowled well enough to make the team and flew directly from there to Fort Huachuca, Arizona, on an Army base to bowl against the Army, Air Force, and Marines. We were treated like royalty. We were taken to the best restaurants in the area and fed the biggest steaks and even golfed on the nicest courses while we were there.

It was 1984, and while I was there, I won All-Service Bowler of the Year for women, which included three gold medals and a bronze medal. At the awards ceremony, a Navy captain, giving out the medals, even kissed me on the cheek three or four times, one kiss for each medal he presented me with. It was almost embarrassing. Then I, including a second-place female, and the first- and second-place males, immediately flew to Las Vegas, Nevada, to bowl in the International Amateur Bowling Tournament in Sam's Town. That was a hotel and bowling lanes in one big building. We were given bowling shirts with the letters USA on the back. Yes, we were representing the United States in this international tournament, which was a precursor to the Olympics. I was very proud and excited to be bowling. Unfortunately, I hurt my knee while I was winning the gold medals, and it was downhill from then on. The pain got excruciating, and my knee swelled up like a balloon, but I wrapped it up and just kept bowling.

As we were sitting down to eat with the other bowlers, one of the coordinators stood up, pointed to each of us, and said, "You are going to the Olympics." I was thrilled. That was my dream goal since I was a little girl. This was going to be the year bowling was introduced to the Olympics and unfortunately the last. Little did I know that my knee would be my downfall and prevent me from going to the Olympics and even bowling for years to come.

The last two days I was there, I made friends with a waitress and let her know I would like to go out and see the lights of Las Vegas. She told me she had a brother who could take us out in his car to see the lights after she got off work. So I waited till she got off work, and her brother came to get her, but he wanted to sit and drink a few shots and gamble a little before we left. I sat there, waiting next to him at the bar, feeling very uncomfortable because I hated gambling, and I didn't want to drink. After about an hour, we finally left; and after getting in the car, he lit up a joint and passed it to his sister, who was on the other side of me. I was upset because I told them I was in the Navy and didn't do that kind of thing anymore. I told them I was trying to quit drinking at that time also. He started the car, and off we went to go look at the lights of the city, but he was going real slow and said he was too high to keep driving. He wanted to stop somewhere; so we stopped at the nearest bar, got out, and went inside. I ended up dancing with her brother all night, and while I was doing that, she met an older guy who said he could rent a boat and take us down the Colorado River. I was very disappointed when I looked out the window and saw the sun coming up, and I hadn't even seen the lights of Las Vegas yet. Well, I had to agree; we might as well go down the Colorado River, since it was morning, and I didn't have a vehicle, and they did.

So off we went in the other guy's car down to the river to rent a boat. We stopped at the hotel along the way to get my bathing suit, and of course they bought a case of beer to bring with us, and we went upstream toward the dam. Along the way, we decided to stop and look at bighorn sheep. Her brother seemed to know the area because he said there were hot springs just up in the hills from where we came ashore. It was a 110 degrees outside, and as they were hiking up toward the hot springs, I decided to cool off by wading in the Colorado River, but I didn't realize how cold the water was. It was close to freezing since it was coming from the bottom of Lake Mead, which is one of the deepest lakes in North America. I went out just waist deep, and all of a sudden, my hands and my feet started cramping up, and I was literally freezing to death. I turned around to go back to shore, and I found myself swimming for my life against the current. I thought I was going to die, but I made it back, barely. Good thing I was an excellent swimmer or I would have drowned for sure. I finally caught up with them hiking up the trail, but they never knew what I had just gone through. When we got to the hot springs, her brother took off all his clothes and jumped in naked. I didn't blame him, but I thought it was kind of weird, and we didn't get to see any bighorn sheep.

Afterward, we walked down back to the boat and drove it up as close to the dam as we could and still be safe. From where we were, the dam looked so massive. Then we turned around and drove the boat back home. We got back the Ford Bronco, and we all piled in exhausted. I was sitting in the front passenger seat. As the older guy was driving along, he said, "I'm too drunk to drive," and asked the waitress, "Can your brother drive?" as he was passed out in the back seat.

And I said, "If he drives, I'm jumping out of the car."

Then he asked the waitress, "Why don't you drive?"

Knowing how much she drank, I said, "If she drives, I'm jumping out of the car." Then I suggested, "Why don't I drive since I haven't had anything to drink and I'm perfectly sober and awake?"

Then he and the waitress both said, "Oh, that sounds like a good idea." So he stopped the car on the side of the road, and I got out and started driving. As we're getting closer to downtown Las Vegas, the waitress decided to take her top off and stand up through the sunroof and flash everybody as we were driving. I thought we were going to get arrested, but thank goodness nobody really saw us or reported us. We finally got back to the hotel where I got out and went back to my room. Boy, was I relieved to be back, alive and in one piece. I couldn't wait to get home. And I never did get to see the lights of Las Vegas that night.

I finally made it back to Mayport, Florida. Home with my family even though home was still in a bedroom with a mattress on the floor. I brought my medals in to work with me to show the captain the next day. He was so proud of me he immediately promoted me to E4 and made me sailor of the month. Then a little later, I made sailor of the quarter and had my own parking place. I was even recommended for sailor of the year. I was runner-up for that. It was kind of weird being somewhat homeless and having my own parking spot at work.

I really liked working in sheet metal shop because even though I was the only female, I was getting along with my fellow sailors at the time, designing and building salad bars and other various jobs for the destroyers in the port. But he thought he was doing me a favor and gave me another job and put me under a chief who didn't like me. All I had to do was walk around the shops and get signatures. I thought it was the most boring job I've ever had. And not very challenging either.

Then came my next and, little did I know, my last bowling tournament in the Navy. They gave me $850 cash and sent me to Niagara Falls to bowl in the queen's tournament, which is a professional tournament.

When I got on the plane to go to Niagara Falls, I sat down next to a state trooper who was with a bunch of other state troopers from that area who came down for a convention. I told the guy next to me what I was going to Niagara Falls for, and he told me he knew a place I could stay for little or nothing. The other guys said I was safe with him, so he took me to his house, and he called the owner of the hotel I was going to stay at and got me a room for $10 a night.

When I got to the hotel, I couldn't believe it. It was called the Hotel Niagara, and it overlooked the falls. It was a suite with chandeliers and everything. I was supposed to stay at the Hilton across town with the other bowlers, but this hotel made the Hilton look like a Motel 6, so I called up the other female bowler and got her to come and stay with me so we could split the room for $5 a night, then we decided to rent a car. They had a special for the bowlers for $10 a day, which we split that too, so my $850 went pretty far. It was a good thing because I didn't win anything bowling, but I did have a good time bowling with the pros.

When I made it back home, my knee was killing me, and I was afraid they would put me out of the Navy, so I didn't say anything and just limped around or tried not to limp as much as possible. Then I got promoted to E5 and was taken out of that boring assignment, with the chief who hated me, and was given a job working with other chiefs, planning jobs for the ships. But I wasn't working for them—I was working with them. I worked there a few months longer, and while working there, we found a house to rent in Mayport. It was nice to get out of that bedroom and that mattress on the floor.

Chapter 11
C School

Soon I made a request for C School, called NDT (nondestructive testing), which would take me to San Diego where I was born for at least six months. I would have learned to x-ray welds on ships and submarines to look for cracks, which would give me an excellent paying job after the Navy. My real dream was to be one of the first women underwater welders, but that eluded me because of my knee and my drinking. I soon left for San Diego, California. I was hoping that my knee would get better or at least not get any worse, but unfortunately, it did get worse. I also had a problem staying sober because I went to study group, and most of the other students were drinking. I discovered that instead of soda machines, they had beer machines in the lounge of every barracks.

I was going to AA meetings, but I was not ready to stay sober yet. I got drunk once and told my sponsor, and she told me to write down what step 1 meant to me. I wrote down my drunk-a-log or what I did when I started drinking at age fourteen to that day. Then I got drunk again. She then told me to write down what step 2 meant to me. So I wrote down from when I was born or what I could remember to what led up to my drinking at age fourteen, including all the things that traumatized me as a little child and as an adult and made me feel why I needed to drink or escape from life. In total, it was sixteen pages front and back. I thought I was doing a step 4 in the twelve steps of Alcoholics Anonymous, but according to the book *Alcoholics Anonymous*, this is not a thorough step 4. I was just skimming the surface. Years later, I would do a thorough and better step 4 and the rest of the 12 steps, which would not only keep me sober years longer, but also give me some sanity in my life. Doing this writing did help me, though temporarily, because it was the last drink I had for the next two years.

I got to see my brother Gary who lived there and was a retired firefighter for the San Diego Fire Department. I decided to buy a motorcycle, but I only rode it two months. After my last drunk, my knee was really hurting, and I asked to be sent back to Jacksonville, Florida, where I could get treatment for it, but I really wanted to concentrate on getting sober also. I took the motorcycle back to the dealership where I bought it; and they took it back, no problem, because I was in the Navy. I then flew back to Jacksonville to be with my family and a new command at NAS JAX Airfield, where I was soon to have knee surgery at the hospital there on the base.

CHAPTER 12

LIMITED DUTY
AT SECURITY

I went directly to the security office at the gate to work. All I had to do was check IDs at first. Then I had surgery and was off work while I was doing rehab for my knee. They didn't find anything wrong with my knee except redness and fluid, which they drained. Then they put me on rigorous therapy, which I thought was a mistake because my knee just kept swelling. I thought they should have immobilized my knee and let it rest for a few weeks and let the tendons heal and then do therapy, but they ruined my knee for the rest of my life. I can bowl for fun now, but I have to wrap it twice with a wrap and a brace, and it still swells.

I worked for security for six months; and one night, we had a plane crash on the landing field, full of pot, which went all over the field. I learned later, it had flown from South America; and running out of fuel, they saw the runway and decided to crash-land on the naval air station in Jacksonville. The next day, I was on the gate checking IDs, and a car pulled up with a young man inside. The car didn't have a military sticker on it, so I asked him for his license and registration. He proceeded to tell me that it was his mother's car, and she was in the hospital on the base, so I had him come in and call the hospital to verify his story. I talked to a lady on the other end who said she was in the hospital, and I asked what room she was in. I was getting suspicious, so I called the hospital myself, and they said they had no such person in there. I wouldn't let him in the gate, and he turned around and tried to crash the gate, so I called the MPs (military police), and he quickly drove away.

We all figured that it was probably somebody trying to get at the pot that was on the base. I'm sure that was it, since it was on the news about the airplane crashing with pot all over the airfield, and he probably thought it was easy to get to on the base. I'm glad my suspicions got the better of me that day. Because of that incident, I thought seriously of becoming a military policewoman, but there was no room in the Navy billets for that. In other words, there were too many military police at that time in the Navy. So I didn't pursue it.

CHAPTER 13

WORKING AT DISASTER PREPAREDNESS

After my six months of limited duty, I was transferred to disaster preparedness on the same base in which I was working in my rate as a hull technician. As an E-5, I was the senior petty officer in charge of storing and maintaining equipment for nuclear, biological, and chemical disasters. I was also in charge of training in decontamination procedures. I worked with one other petty officer, and we had a commander in charge of us who flew helicopters. A couple of times, he took us down to Homestead, Florida, a naval base near Miami, for lunch and back. It was about a one-hour flight. I loved dangling my feet out the door of the helicopter and counting the swimming pools on the way down. Of course I was tethered in so I wouldn't fall out. We wore flight suits and a helmet that had all kinds of radio noise while we were flying. It was exciting.

One time on the way back, we flew through a thunder and lightning storm. The helicopter shook as the thunder roared around us, and the lightning was so close it was blinding. I thought we were going to have to make an emergency landing or even crash, but we landed safely thanks be to God and the skill of our commander because I was praying the whole time.

Another six months had gone by, and I had orders for a submarine tender in Pascagoula, Mississippi. Unfortunately, I started smoking so I could quit drinking, something like replacing one addiction for another. Unfortunately, I got sick, real sick. It was a combination of bronchitis and asthma, and I ended up in the hospital. They diagnosed me with asthma and sent me home on high doses of prednisone. Some kind of steroid. I was hallucinating all night. After a day or two, I went to the doctor and I was put back on limited duty for another six months.

Chapter 14

Limited Duty at Urinalysis

I was sent to work in urinalysis where they have sailors pee in a cup and test them for drugs. Pretty easy duty, but you have to pay attention to detail because you cannot be dyslexic, and transposing numbers can cost a person their career. That's why we always checked the Social Security numbers on the cup with another person. I worked for a First-Class Petty Officer Bellanger and a Chief Myers alongside another female petty officer.

January 28, 1986. I woke up that morning and went to work like every other morning. But it was extremely cold, especially for Florida weather. It must have been down in the thirties. Around noon, I went to get lunch that day for the rest of the crew at a little pizzeria down the street, still on the base. I was waiting at the counter for my order when a guy abruptly came in yelling, "The space shuttle just blew up!" Everyone in the place anxiously went outside and looked up into the sky, and what I saw will be etched in my mind even to this day. I saw the smoke plumes separating from the space shuttle itself. Of course they've shown it on television over and over and over again, but seeing it in person makes it a lot more surreal. I was in shock. I couldn't believe that that was happening. And it seemed like it was right above us. All I could think about was that innocent schoolteacher, Christa McAuliffe, up there wanting to go into space in an adventure of a lifetime. Of course it was dangerous, but we hadn't had any real catastrophes up to that point with the space shuttle program. "Why now, God?" was all I could ask myself. I got the lunch and took it back to the office as fast as I could. When I got there, we turned on the television, which we usually didn't even watch at all, and we all saw what actually happened on TV. It took us a couple of weeks to pretty much stop talking about it, but I know we were all thinking about it quite a bit.

One day, Petty Officer Bellanger asked me if I knew how to play an instrument; and I told him, "I used to play the drums in high school." He said he had a little fife and drum contingent, and next time they practiced, he would like me to come and play a little. I said, "Okay, but it's been a long time since I played." I didn't want to tell him that in high school, in Seattle, I had five classes of music: band, marching band, orchestra, all-city orchestra, and all-city marching band; but I didn't want to say anything because it had been so long since I played any music at all. So when I got there, they handed me a pair of sticks and said, "Go ahead and see if you could play." I played a little, and they said, "Okay, we'll teach you the rest on the way to New Orleans this weekend."

So this was the first time I was drafted in the Navy. They had uniforms depicting the 1700s: red-and-white striped shirts and black flat hats with white bell-bottom pants and wide black belts. We also had black silk kerchiefs around our necks. It looked pretty authentic. None of us had any idea that this little contingent would go as far as it would for our country. Our main aim was to play for retirement and/or reenlistment ceremonies around the country. Working on an air base had its advantages because, of course, we needed rides to these activities around the country; so conveniently, we would borrow a P-3 Orion, which was a spy plane used to detect Russian submarines (called Bears in military terms) off the East Coast of the United States.

One day, Chief Myers came in, all excited, and it took a lot to get him excited, and he told us, "We are invited to play for the president of the United States in the Statue of Liberty ceremony in New York City." I couldn't believe it! What an honor! Not everyone gets to play an instrument for a dignitary like Queen Elizabeth, but to play for her and the president of the United States is just unheard of. I felt very humbled because it wasn't like bowling where I practiced and planned to be the best at something like that. This was just being in the right place at the right time just because I played the drums. Well, soon we were on our way to New York City. Once we landed, we got in a school bus, which took us across town to our new home away from home: the *Intrepid*, a retired World War II aircraft carrier that had actually become a museum ship. I don't know how the sailors slept on the ships in World War II because the bunks were stacked four high and with very thin mattresses. We had to spend a week up there, and I thought I was going to die by the time it was over. I was still pretty out of shape from being sick and in the hospital a few weeks before.

Every day we had to get up at five thirty in the morning and be transported across New York Harbor by a Liberty boat to and from our destination. Some days we wouldn't make it back from practice till after midnight. So we didn't get much sleep. First we would go to the USS *Kennedy* to practice, and then we were allowed to go and play for a parade that was in town, which wasn't planned. Then one day, we played for the opening ceremony of the New York Mets game. I'm not sure if that was planned. We even brought our own photographer to capture it all on camera. We got there early to play in the pregame ceremony, and as they were warming up, I got a baseball signed by some of the Mets team. This was the year they went on to win the World Series. I lost that ball in Hurricane Charley, years later, in Florida with all the pictures that the photographer took and almost everything I owned. But that's another story.

We only had one day that we could go out for a little R&R and eat at a fine restaurant and do some sightseeing. We also went to Times Square and got some pictures of the Twin Towers. I noticed as we rode the big yellow school bus across town and over the Brooklyn

Bridge, there was absolutely no other traffic on the road. The whole city was shut down to outside traffic because the president was there. I've never been to New York before, but I've seen it on TV, and I never saw it so empty without a lot of people or cars. It was kind of eerie. Unlike being on land, the New York Harbor was so crowded with boats that it was hard to navigate the Liberty boat we rode in. And because of it, the waves were pretty nasty too. Good thing nobody got seasick. At least I didn't. I was used to it because I grew up with a retired Navy father who took us salmon fishing out on Puget Sound in Seattle in small craft warnings with three kids and two adults in a sixteen-foot ski boat. So I learned not to get seasick or to live without complaining.

After a week of practicing, the day finally came to play for the president. I knew we were ready to give the performance of a lifetime, and I couldn't believe they put me and the other drummers in the front row, and because of it, when we did the performance, I was looking eye to eye with President Reagan and Nancy Reagan with Brooke Shields sitting right behind them.

We thought with all the practicing we did, nothing would go wrong. The American Marine Band was on the left of us, and the Royal British Marine Band was on the right of us facing each other, and we were on a stage in the middle facing the president. The conductor was facing us with his stick in his hand. He raised it up for the fife and drum corps to play first, and as he raised it, suddenly the Royal British Marine Band started playing out of turn. I couldn't believe it after all that practice. Then the conductor put his arms down and waited for them to finish, and then he directed us to play the next song, which went flawlessly after that, and I don't think the president knew any different. We were all shocked how those tough British would let their nerves get the best of them and be the ones to make a mistake, especially since they were professionals and we weren't. Well, the rest of it went off without a hitch, in spite of the British. By the time we were done, I was exhausted and ready to come home. I was still feeling the effects of the asthma and bronchitis I had a few weeks earlier because sometimes I felt like I was going to collapse, but I persevered through it all, and it was worth it. It was an experience of a lifetime.

After getting back to Jacksonville and a regular work routine, Ollie and I decided to buy a brand-new mobile home and move into a mobile home park where First Class Petty Officer Jameson, whom I was working with in security, was living. So we had someone we knew as a neighbor. In fact, there were a lot of military people in the mobile home park that we lived at.

A few months later, the rest of my six-month limited duty in urinalysis came to an end, and because I was well enough, it was time for me to either get out of the Navy or reenlist. Since they offered me a $20,000 reenlistment bonus, I decided to reenlist. And I did it in style: in my fife-and-drum uniform. It was a nice little ceremony in the office with a cake. And my family was there also. I got my orders, and it was to a ship in Norfolk, Virginia, called the USS *Shenandoah*, a destroyer tender.

CHAPTER 15

MY NEXT ENLISTMENT

I had about thirty days' leave to go ahead and move my mobile home up to where I found a mobile home park in Gloucester Point, Virginia, right next to Petty Officer Jameson, whom I used to work with in security. He and his wife moved his mobile home up there, where he got orders to a ship in Norfolk but unfortunately not the *Shenandoah*. At least we had neighbors we knew and were friends with. That always makes it easier when you're moving around, which is what the military is all about.

I thought moving a mobile home would be cheaper and easier because they give you so much money to move a mobile for their enlisted people, and it's better than just moving up there and buying a house. By the time we got everything settled in, including the mobile home, moved, and secured in our new place, we ended up spending all of the $20,000, plus we ended up going into debt.

We found out later why we owed the government extra money for moving us. It was because the mobile home moving company flattened seven tires on the way up to Gloucester Point. When we bought the mobile home, they were supposed to store the new tires that went with it and use them to move it, but we found out later that they just used old tires to move it and probably sold the new ones and made a profit. Either way, they charged the government for moving us almost $1,000 a tire extra, plus the amount it cost to move the mobile home, and those were seven tires they blew on the way up. It was outrageous, but we couldn't fight it because they charged the government the money, and they paid it, so we had to pay the extra back to the government. What a rip-off. That was just the beginning of the stress that I had going to the ship for the first time. I had no idea it was going to last two and a half years and affect me for the rest of my life.

CHAPTER 16
GETTING TO THE SHIP

After my leave was over and I was somewhat settled into our new place, I finally reported on board to my new command. I didn't realize when I moved up there how far the ship was from where we were actually living. It was close to fifty miles away, and not only that, I had to go over two bridges and through a tunnel. I don't just think, I know that the driving and traffic jams that I endured over those next few years had a lot to do with my ultimate stress level. Not only that but after just two weeks of being on board, the ship had to go to the yards up in Baltimore, Maryland, for a complete refit for four months. That meant I had to drive back and forth on weekends because the one-way trip was a three-hour drive. It probably wouldn't have been as bad if I had been accepted where I worked on the ship. I was put in the carpenter shop, which seemed nice because it was fairly clean and not really too hard work; but unfortunately (being the only female in the shop), things went from bad to worse after Petty Officer Bradley (same rank as I was) kept hitting on me (or asking me out).

He first asked me out, and I told him I was married. Then he asked me out again, and I said I was happily married. I guess he didn't like rejection because he treated me like dirt after that. He had been there longer, so I just assumed that he was in charge, and I allowed him to treat me badly by making me swab the deck in front of the E-1s and up. Looking back at it now, I should not have allowed that to happen. I should have delegated that kind of duty to the lower-ranked personnel. But I guess that was the female in me, being the subordinate to the male, which was a mistake on my part and something you just don't do in the military. Since I was new to this shipboard environment, I guess I was very fearful of making enemies. And there were only three hundred females to a thousand males on board. I could tell Chief Rodinez, who was in charge of the shop, was against women being on ships also; and when he saw the way I was being treated by Petty Officer Bradley, he encouraged it even more. I noticed they were giving me jobs to do that kept me up all night like cleaning and maintenance of the machinery every night for the whole week, and then on the weekends, I would have to drive home. They were trying to either break me or see if I would fall asleep on my way home and kill myself. Either way, it was a very bad situation.

A couple of weeks after getting to the shipyards, I went to indoc-trination class, and they were talking to us about sexual harassment and sexual discrimination, and I asked them, "What do you do if that happens?" I explained to them a little of what I was going through, and they told me, "All you can do is document it." I don't think they really knew what to do about it because we, as women, were new to ships. We were in all-new territory. Well, from then on, that's what I did. I documented it, including names, dates, times, everything. I didn't realize it at the time, but there was a division officer behind everything being done to me. And that was Chief Warrant Officer Murdock. He was an old salt who definitely didn't want women on ships and was bound and determined not to let it happen by making me the bad example. Little did he know he was going against prog-ress, and that was the future of the Navy. All I wanted was to make the Navy my career. And I thought because the guys showed me some respect in my first enlistment, the ship would be just as good.

One day, I was off work, and I decided to go snow skiing with a fellow sailor. As we were skiing, he pulled a flask of Blackberry Brandy out of his coat pocket. I told him, "I haven't had a drink in almost two years," and I was very proud of it at the time. I said, "In fact, my anniversary is in two days." He put the flask away until we were in the car and driving back to the ship. I got a little scared, thinking that we could get caught with alcohol in the car in the parking lot; so I told him to hide it down on the floorboards, as we went through the gate. Well, he left it in my car and went back to the ship ahead of me, and I decided to take it out of the car and put it in front of the car on the ground. I looked at it as I walked away, thinking, *Just one sip wouldn't hurt me.* So I took a swig of it and put it back on the ground, and as I was walking away, I thought to myself, *See, I can take it or leave it.* Well, that was the start of another obsession.

I felt like I deserved a good time because of all the crap I had been through, so I was off again the next day and decided to go out on the town. I got some friends, and we shared a cab and went out to eat. We went to a place where you could drink and decided to have a few beers, and that's all it took. I even told the cabdriver I would buy him drinks if he turned off the counter. Then all I remember was some of the girls dragging me into the berthing area of the ship (where we slept) and to my rack, and when I woke up the next morning, it seemed just like when I was back in boot camp. Everybody was mad at me. It was because a couple of the girls were the same ones whom I went to boot camp with. It was déjà vu. I felt very ashamed of myself again. I know my relapse had a lot to do with moving and not getting established in AA meetings like I had been in Florida. After being sober thirty-two years now and looking back on it, if I had been working the program of Alcoholics Anonymous, I would not have been as fearful and would have been able to handle myself in any situation. At any rate, it was like throwing a kitten into a pack of wolves. I thought I was able to handle myself with guys because I was brought up by my brother, Rick, who on many occasions beat me up and never treated me with kid gloves. More like a punching bag.

From then on, I tried to make more meetings in Baltimore. I even got a husband and wife to be my sponsors. It was hard to make meetings at home in Gloucester because I had to get up early at three fifteen in the morning to be at the ship by six or six thirty so that I can make muster at seven. I just didn't want to make the time to stay up till nine or ten o'clock at night going to the meetings. I had little or no sleep. That was the excuse I made to myself why I didn't stay sober.

Four months had gone by, and the ship was finally done with the refit and ready to go out for a trial run. Everybody on board was excited and ready to get back home to Norfolk, Virginia. The weekend before the ship was going to leave, we were at home in Gloucester, and we carpooled with a few other sailors so we wouldn't leave our cars up in Baltimore, but there was a big snowstorm that hit the whole northeast area. We had to drive through about four feet of snow the whole way. It was pretty scary driving, but we had a good driver, and we made it back successfully even though it took about six hours of steady but slow driving. This was the Nor'easter of 1986, as they called it. One of the worst storms in history.

CHAPTER 17

MY FIRST CRUISE

After we got back, I went to bed that night thinking I would get up the next morning and get ready to leave the yards; but during the night, we were all in for a big surprise. Early the next morning, when I woke up, I looked down and saw about two feet of water. The heads (or toilets) backed up and flooded the whole berthing area with contaminated water. I was still smoking at the time, and I had just bought two cartons of cigarettes and left them on the deck (or floor). I was in the second rack (or bunk) up, so I didn't get wet myself, but I watched $20 in cigarettes just floating, and nothing I could do about it. If it couldn't be washed, it all had to be thrown away because it was contaminated. By the next day, it was all pretty well cleaned up, and we were ready to leave port. Little did we know that there was a nor'easter in the making out in the North Atlantic, and we were headed right for it. Our captain knew though. In fact, he headed straight for the middle of it. His nickname was Mad Jack. And we found out that he used to be a submariner, but he didn't wear any dolphins, which is a pin submariners wear. In fact, my father wore them because he was a submariner in World War II. We found out that our captain, Mad Jack, had them taken away because when he was captain of a submarine, he accidentally came up underneath a destroyer, and he was demoted to commanding our ship.

Needless to say, there were rough seas, and they got rougher as the night wore on. And because he wanted to see how well his ship would hold up, he was going full throttle the whole way. While we're eating on the mess decks, we had to hold on to our trays so they

71

wouldn't roll off the table. For my initiation to the first time at sea, the guys in the shop wanted to see if I would go which sick, so they got me my food, which was a mixture of different foods piled onto my plate including chicken, ice cream with gravy on it, and even spaghetti. And to top it all off, they put hot sauce on all of it. The Navy is based on a lot of traditions, including initiations, and that's why I played along and ate the food. And I didn't get sick. It doesn't mean that I didn't feel nauseous, but I didn't actually throw up. I think they were starting to accept me because of this.

Before going to bed, I went toward the front of the ship to see the waves crashing over the bow and I saw a poor female wearing an overcoat and a hat, totally drenched, hanging on to a railing in the middle of the bow, facing forward. Her job was a lookout to make sure we didn't run into any other ships or to see lighthouses in the distance. I felt so sorry for her as she was getting hit by all the huge waves coming over the bow. Suddenly, I saw two other sailors going out to her, and I thought they were bringing her inside, but no, they were tying her to the railing with ropes so she wouldn't be swept overboard. I thought that was outrageous, but it had to be done, and I was glad it wasn't me. That was a boatswain's mate's job, and I was an HT (hull tech). Later on, I went to bed, and because our berthing was toward the front of the ship, all night long I felt the ship lifting up and then come crashing down with a big boom as it went over each wave. The waves must have been at least 40 feet high, and the ship was approximately 650 feet long. Each bunk had two leather straps that hooked up and down on the outside to keep you from falling out of bed. I'm glad of that, but needless to say, I didn't get much sleep because it's hard to sleep while you're holding on for dear life.

Morning came; and with the storm finally over, we chugged along, on smoother seas, down to Norfolk, Virginia. We heard some scuttlebutt going around that the captain wanted to go into the eye of the hurricane; but the other officers threatened him that if he made them go into the eye, he wouldn't come out, "alive," that is. Knowing about that captain, to this day, I believed what I heard was true. He was nuts, and he really didn't care about his crew; hence the nickname Mad Jack.

Well, we made it back to Norfolk but not like we thought. Instead of pulling up to the pier so we could get off the ship, we anchored out away from the pier and couldn't figure out why. Then we found out that we had to go back to the yards because, going through all that stormy weather, with the ship bouncing all over the place, the shaft to the screw (or propeller) somehow got bent. Whatever it was, it was making a humming sound. They called it a singing screw. Everybody on board was so disappointed we couldn't go ashore. Our families were upset also because they were waiting on the pier for us. So after spending one night anchored away from the pier, we headed back to the yards.

When we got there, we spent that night and the next day while they checked to see if they could fix it. They said they couldn't do anything because it wasn't bent bad enough to hurt the ship's propulsion, so we packed up and left the yards the next morning and went back to Norfolk, but this time in better weather. What made it even worse, when we got back to Norfolk, no one was allowed to leave the ship. It was like we were in prison, and we were being punished for some reason. In fact, the captain ordered all hands to clean the ship with toothbrushes, officers included. Everybody called our captain Captain Bligh. We were listening to the radio as we were cleaning, and we heard the disc jockey say to the whole world, "Our condolences go out to the crew of the *Shenandoah* because they have to clean the ship with toothbrushes and can't even go home to their families." It wasn't till the next day we were allowed to go home.

Chapter 18
Our New Captain

Not surprisingly, we were soon gifted with a new captain, and his name was Captain Wright. Everyone on board was ecstatic to see the other captain go and eager to see what kind of captain we had now. We knew he couldn't be any worse than the last one and hopefully much better for the future of our ship and crew. While we were at Norfolk, we went out on two- to three-day cruises almost every other week. We were constantly doing drills and training, training, training besides our regular work. The whole ship would do man-overboard drills at least once every time we went out. When we were at general quarters, I was in charge of a group of sailors in nuclear, chemical, and biological training and how to wear a gas mask. I did this while I was working in the carpenter shop.

One day, Chief Rodinez put me in charge of a crew to do a job of painting the deck and the lines around the machinery in the shop. It sounded simple enough, but it involved a lot of time because we had to tape off the lines around the machinery, and there was a lot of machinery. The problem was, we started late in the afternoon after work, and the job had to be done by the next morning. I think he knew what was going to happen because with his orders, he said, "If this job is not completed by morning, you will be put on report." Well, during the night while we were working, I knew that if we kept painting, it wouldn't be dry by morning, and then we wouldn't be able to work our regular jobs with the machines, so I gave the order to stop and go to bed. No surprise, I was put on report and sent to the division officer. I tried to explain the situation, but he didn't care to hear it, probably because they planned it in the first place. My punishment was to clean the shop and all the machines every night after regular working hours for one week. I couldn't even go home to see my family. That was the last straw. When I finally got home, I told my husband to write our congressman and let him know that I was being sexually discriminated against and how I was being treated.

After that, I happened to be transferred to another shop, called lagging (or insulation). I know that the division officer thought he was putting me in a worse situation to break me, but it backfired on him because it turned out that I loved it. I was put second in charge of insulating the pipes and bulkheads (or walls). There was a first-class petty officer in charge of the shop, not a chief, and I got along with him pretty well. They used to use asbestos for insulating the ships, but then they changed to fiberglass, and it was very itchy to work with. We did have to remove asbestos from some of the older ships, and with that, we had to put on complete bodysuits with face masks and air hoses for protection. I got to work with a sewing machine, which I learned to use in high school. I even made a lot of my own clothes back then. I was amazed on how well some of the guys knew how to run a sewing machine.

I loved crawling around the inside of ships in smaller areas where only I could fit and wrap the pipes. I think the guys appreciated my small size, but a couple of them were very crude and let me know that they didn't like working with women by their vulgar language and explicit talk about sexual matters. I didn't say anything. I just let them talk and let it go over my head. It was still much better than the carpenter shop. That was a very boring place compared to this. In the other shop, we never left the shop or the ship. All we did was make wooden plaques and picture frames, oil the machines, and clean, clean, clean. In the lagging shop, a lot of times, we had to go aboard other ships to repair them; and that was exciting to me. We also worked on different areas of our ship. All the way from the staterooms at the top to down in the engine and boiler (or fire) rooms. We only worked in our shop when we had to sew the fiberglass mats together. For the next couple of months, I was going to be working alongside the crew learning that trade. After the first class thought

I was confident enough, I was put in charge and supervising more than working and never swabbed the deck, like I did in the carpenter shop.

Then one day, a young seaman refused to work for me because, as he said it, "I won't take orders from any cunt." And he said it right in front of the first-class petty officer in charge of the shop. Well, the first class looked at me and said, "How are you going to take that? Are you going to put him on report? Because if you don't, I will!" Needless to say, I definitely put him on report and sent him to captain's mast. It's navy terms, like going to court with just the captain. There, he can ask for a court-martial which would be in front of a judge and jury. But he declined the court-martial. I couldn't believe it! He ruined his career just because he didn't want to work for a woman.

When he went to the captain's mast, the captain asked him, "What are you going to do when you get out of the Navy and go to work for a woman?"

He said, "I won't work for a woman even on the outside."

The captain then said, "Well, you're out of the Navy now." I'm sure someday he'll get a rude awakening and realize the world is changing. At least I hope so.

CHAPTER 19
LIBERTY IN THE BAHAMAS

Pretty soon we were on our way to Cuba; but we got to make a stop at Freeport, in the Bahamas, for three days, which happened to be on the way. We were on three-section duty, so that gave each duty section at least two days to go out and have a good time. What a difference between this captain and the captain we had before. Captain Wright seemed to really take care of his crew. When I was on duty in port, I spent four hours on the quarterdeck, which was at the top of the gangplank where people came to check into the ship, with a loaded .45 on my hip. If there were any emergencies, I was the one who announced it over the loudspeaker throughout the ship. In my first enlistment, right after A school, I went to the rifle range, and I got a marksman ribbon shooting with the pistol. At eight years old, my father used to take us down to the garbage dump and let us shoot rats with his pistol, so I definitely knew how to shoot. I remember back in those days, my hero was Annie Oakley. When we were at sea, we would practice shooting the rifle at targets set up on the stern or back of the ship.

When we pulled into Freeport, I arranged a sightseeing tour with ten other sailors, and it was really nice. We got to see quite a bit of the island with a Bohemian guide. Most of the other sailors went out and got drunk because the rum was so cheap there. I saw one sailor being carried off a bus, and all I could think about was *Thank goodness that's not me.*

Right after being transferred to the lagging shop, I was also transferred to a firefighting damage control team during general quarters drills. There was an on-scene leader, there was an assistant on-scene leader, and then there was me. I was put in charge of the hose teams. When there was a drill, we met in front of the engine room, and I made sure that my people were manning the hoses and ready to turn the water on. It seemed we were doing drills constantly, at least once or twice a week. We were almost able to do it in our sleep. Little did I know that this was going to be the most important job on the ship and a matter of life or death later on.

CHAPTER 20
ON OUR WAY TO CUBA

After the liberty and fun we had in the Bahamas, we set sail to Gitmo (short for Guantanamo Bay, Cuba) and war games. This was the Cold War remember, and we had to be ready for anything, including war. We were there two weeks, and I was still working with the crew and learning my trade. I enjoyed it because after we pulled into port, we had to go to another ship and insulate some of the pipes down in their engine room.

The next day, we left port to do war games with our sister ship, the *Yellowstone*. As we were leaving the harbor, we almost hit a Russian trawler, or to put it truthfully, they almost hit us. We came within a few feet of hitting them; and I heard that if the captain of a Russian ship hits an American ship, they're promoted, whereas our captains are demoted or transferred usually.

After we got out into open sea, our ships were circling each other, including our sister ship and a couple of other destroyers. As we were coming around, I noticed that we were going straight for the *Yellowstone*, and I didn't think they had time to get out of our way. I thought for sure we were going to collide. Suddenly, our captain, who was a brilliant navigator, took the helm and turned the wheel of our massive ship. As we got closer to the *Yellowstone*, we were so close we could hear them sound the collision alarm and their loudspeaker say, "All hands brace for impact." I saw everyone on their ship lie down flat on the deck. But our captain didn't even sound our alarm, and as we rumbled by them just a few feet away, we thumbed our noses at them. Talk about playing games. I loved the Navy so much;

and when they called it war games, it seemed like a game, only more serious and sometimes dangerous, but very exciting. I wanted to stay in for life; but unfortunately, if it wasn't for some of the old salts making it hard for women to be on ships, it would have been my life.

We went out on maneuvers several times more while we were there, and when we weren't out at sea, we were working on our ship or another ship that needed repairing. There were only a couple of days we got to spend on liberty, and to this day, I wish I had never gone out. We were actually anchored out away from the pier, so we had to take a liberty launch back and forth to shore or to other ships to work.

One day, I decided to go out with some of the other girls; but once we got to shore, they got in a cab and said, "You don't want to go with us because we're going out drinking." These were the same girls who carried me in the last time I got drunk, and obviously they didn't want to carry me in again. Feeling lonely and dejected, I decided to walk over to the Chiefs Club, since it was close by; and as I was looking through the fence in the pool area, one of the chiefs invited me to come in. I told him I wasn't a chief, and he said, "Don't worry, you could be my guest." Well, as a female in pretty good shape (only a hundred and ten pounds soaking wet), I guess I looked pretty attractive to him. I knew I was married, but I was still lonely and just wanted somebody to talk to. I had my bathing suit on under my clothes ready to go swimming at either the pool or the beach, so I stripped my clothes off and jumped in the pool since it was ninety-seven degrees outside, and I was already hot and sweaty.

As I was relaxing by the poolside, he asked me, "Say, would you like some sun lotion rubbed on your back?"

And having a few drinks in me already, I said, "Sure, why not." At this time, I was thinking he was getting a little too friendly, so I asked him, "Where's the beach?" He told me how to get there, so I decided to leave the pool area and go down to the beach and see what that's like. By this time, I had quite a few beers in me and was pretty lit up. Along the way, I met another chief and two enlisted guys with him, and I asked them where the beach was. They said, "Don't worry, we'll show you." Well, we walked down to the beach and found a lot of large rocks and not very sandy. It reminded me of the Pacific Northwest but extremely hot. All of a sudden, one of the enlisted guys, being almost as drunk as I was, pulled me down behind a rock and tried to strip me. As I was trying to fight him off, his friend came over and acted like he was helping me; and when I got up, he grabbed me and started to kiss me and said, "It's okay. I'm here to save you."

At first, the chief was just standing there watching the whole thing, and then he decided to help me, and as he pulled the guy away, he said, "No, she doesn't want to, so just leave her alone," and then he started kissing me. That's when I pushed him away and ran as fast as I could back to the Chiefs Club, where I got my clothes on and had a few more drinks and finally went back to the ship. As I was getting into the liberty boat, I was pretty drunk, and as I was sitting down on the bottom of the boat, I remember looking up at some of the other sailors standing above me, who knew me from before, and I felt so humiliated and ashamed. This was to be my last drunk. Not my last drink, but definitely my last drunk. The next day, I woke up with not only a hangover, but also a very bad sunburn that was a third-degree burn on the back of my neck. It even left a scar, which I deserved.

After our last maneuver off the coast of Cuba, which went without incident, it was time to head back to Norfolk and get ready for the Med cruise. That's what we were preparing for anyway. I couldn't wait to get back home because I missed my family so much. And I knew we'd have to head out again on a much longer cruise. When we got back, I was getting in my car, and I noticed the screen on the front of my car was in the trunk and all torn up. So I asked my husband, "What happened to this?" pointing to my screen, and he told me they got in a car accident while I was gone. Thank goodness they weren't hurt, but they knew I would get angry, so they were trying to hide it from me. I didn't get angry. I just got very upset because, in a way, I felt guilty because I knew my drinking, which I didn't tell them about, and the car accident were connected somehow. I felt that when I didn't drink, God's hand is over us and protecting us, but when I did drink or get drunk, He lifts His hand and allows anything to happen, and it did. To this day, I have never told them about what happened in Cuba.

CHAPTER 21

SETTING SAIL TO THE MEDITERRANEAN

The day came when we had to leave for the Mediterranean. My husband and daughter drove me down to the pier where they were having a big celebration for the departure of our ship and the other ships included in the whole battle group. You would think that Sunny was used to my leaving a lot, but I could tell she was very sad, knowing I would be gone possibly the next six months. When I gave her a big hug, I didn't want to let her go. I gave Ollie a big hug and a kiss and said my goodbyes and started up the gangplank. Saying goodbye to my family was the hardest part of being in the Navy, but it was the life I chose. I remember as a child I had to go through the same thing when my father had to leave and go on deployments for six months at a time, and I remember waiting on the pier with my mother and sister and brother when his ship came in. Even though I was very young, I was very proud of my father, and I remember in the back of my mind that maybe someday I could do the same thing, but I never thought it would actually come true because I was a girl, and girls don't get to do things like that. I found out that dreams do come true. And mine did.

As we were pulling away from the pier, we were all in our dress whites manning the rails. I stood there at parade rest feeling as proud as I could be, and I'm sure it looked really awesome from the crowds below as we left port. This was the beginning of July, and we thought we would be gone through to the next Christmas because up till now all Med cruises have been six-month deployments or more.

Once we got out into open water, we had our usual man-overboard drill where we all had to muster (or gather) outside on the upper deck toward the middle of the ship near the lifeboats, and I had to instruct the others in my group on how we were to abandon ship if the ship was sinking. The next morning, as we did every morning at seven o'clock (in port as well as at sea), the repair department mustered in our usual place in the cargo handling passageway. (That's where they store a lot of sheet metal, which is tack welded up right so that it won't fall down.) We lined up right in front of it, and they called out our names to be counted so they can tell if anyone is UA (unauthorized absence) or has fallen overboard. Then we went to our shops to work as usual.

This particular day, the day after leaving port, we were to replace insulation in the captain's stateroom. We brought our radio, as we usually did when we're working, and I was listening to the music as I looked out the porthole. It was the kind of music in tune with the rocking of the ship in six-foot swells. From the view of the stateroom, I could see the oiler behind us, moving slightly faster, trying to catch up. It was called a VERTREP (vertical replenishment), where we get refueled at sea. It seemed like it took hours for the oiler to inch its way closer till, finally, we were side by side. Finished with my work, I went topside to see the action firsthand. It was awesome to watch. With the two ships only a few feet apart, doing about twenty knots, someone on the oiler started the process by shooting a line with a gun over to us. I was amazed to watch the boatswain's mates, the backbone of the Navy, all working together like a finely tuned watch. Men and women, side by side, were pulling in the lines and hooking up the pipelines with the ease and dexterity of acrobats. Finally, they unhooked the lines; and with the last flexible pipe, being pulled in by the oiler, we waved goodbye and started to separate. My heart felt like it was going to burst with pride knowing that our Navy is the only Navy in the world to replenish at sea, and I was a part of it.

FILL IT UP

After a couple of days, the six-foot swells smoothed out into a sea of glass. It was amazing. There wasn't even a ripple in the water. The only waves that were made was by us and the battle group that was following us. I couldn't believe it, being out in middle of the Atlantic Ocean with not even a tiny ripple in the water. This was a far cry from the first time I went out into a nor'easter with the waves forty feet high. It was going to take us two whole weeks to get across the ocean, because we were taking our time getting to Europe, for some reason. Possibly to keep doing training and drills. Besides fire drills, we also had to do security drills, which we made a game out of. It was somewhat dangerous because if caught moving around the ship, you could be shot. The alarm would sound, and they would say, "Security alert, security alert, all hands stand fast." This was a way of catching intruders or spies, and the masters-at-arms (or military police at sea) would run around the ship with their guns drawn, ready to shoot anyone that moved. If I wasn't on the mess decks, I would slowly make my way there so I could sit and have a cup of coffee while I was waiting for the "security alert" to be over.

I've always had a split personality to where, on the one hand, I would be very conscientious of the rules, but on the other hand, when no one in authority was looking, I'd play the bad girl and try to get away with as much as I could, without being caught. That was my alcoholic personality taking charge. I thought it was my fun side. Life seemed boring otherwise, as long as nobody got hurt. I think I learned that from my brother Rick, who was our (me and my younger sisters) babysitter after my elder brother and sister left home. He was only four years older than I was and had quite a sense of humor, but he also had a sadistic side, because he liked to hurt us a lot physically as well as emotionally and mentally. I believe he instilled in me a tomboy personality and toughened me up quite a bit too.

After a week in the middle of the North Atlantic, we had a luau on the upper deck. It was wild. I never thought we could have fun and just let loose like that on the ship, especially after Mad Jack. They had a pig roast and all kinds of food prepared for us. They allowed a can of beer for each of us, but I declined. I knew I wouldn't be able to get drunk, but I still wanted to stop drinking, especially after what happened in Gitmo. Fortunately, the food was phenomenal because our galley had some of the finest chefs in the Navy on board. We fed other ships when their galley or mess decks were being repaired, and they loved it.

Because the weather was so nice and sunny every day on the way to the Med, a couple of times after work, another girl and I would sneak topside, in our bathing suits, and find a secret place where no one knew about and sunbathe. It was such a big ship, you could get away with just about anything. A couple of times during the Med cruise, they found two sailors making out in remote parts of the ship. There were so many cracks and crevices they could hide in. Because of it, they started calling our ship the Love Boat. Unfortunately, that's why the "old salts" didn't want women on ships, but times change, and they should accept that.

One day, as we were chugging along, I suddenly felt the ship vibrate. I had a weird feeling about what had just happened. Then I heard over the loudspeaker that we had hit a whale, or maybe the whale hit us, but either way, we killed it, and it was a tragic incident. We had to notify the authorities in charge of animal rights and let them know about it. The next day, after two weeks of seeing nothing but blue sky and empty flat water, I was looking over the bow of the ship, and all of a sudden, on the starboard (or right side) of the ship, I noticed dolphins jumping out of the water, and then I looked over to the port (or left side) and noticed a single-masted sailboat. It seemed like we were out in the middle of nowhere, but we were actually getting close to the Azores, a group of islands in the North Atlantic, which meant we were getting closer to Europe. It was about time. Then we started seeing other ships like tankers and such. We were in the shipping lanes, and soon we were near the Straits of Gibraltar. Because the straits are narrow, as we were passing by the Rock of Gibraltar, we had to be careful not to hit other ships, including a Russian submarine that was partially submerged right next to us. It's not every day you get to see a Russian submarine, especially that close.

CHAPTER 22

FIRST PORT OF CALL

After entering the Mediterranean Sea, we pulled into our first liberty port: Palma de Mallorca, Spain. This is an island off the coast of Spain, which is a vacation spot for the Europeans, but mostly the British. We were all anxious to go ashore, since we had been out to sea for two whole weeks, with nothing but open water around us. I noticed some of the girls getting ready to go out, and I asked them if I could go with them, and they said, "No, we're going out drinking, and you really don't want to go with us." They meant well, because they knew I was trying to quit drinking, and I'm sure they didn't want to carry me back in again like last time, but I still felt dejected, so I went out by myself.

I went down near the beach and found a nice little restaurant with chairs outside, so I sat down to eat lunch. I asked for a steak and a soda, but I had to send the steak back because it was so rare I couldn't eat it. The waiter felt bad, so he brought me a small glass of champagne. I took a long look at it and knew that I shouldn't drink it, but I didn't want to offend the waiter, so I drank it down. I instantly felt guilty, so I went to the nearest hotel. Thank goodness the people in the lobby spoke English since they were British. I felt kind of embarrassed, but I asked them about Alcoholics Anonymous. They handed me a phone book; and I found, right in the beginning of it, Alcoholics Anonymous. So I called the number, and a lady answered, and I asked about an AA meeting. I thought it strange; but she asked me, in a British accent, if I knew how to ballroom dance. I said, "No, I sure don't."

She said, "Don't worry, tonight at 6:00 p.m., you just meet us at the hotel near the pier, the one with the big windows in the front. We'll be sitting in a booth inside the restaurant. Just try not to drink till then."

I said, "No problem, I'll meet you there." I just couldn't figure out what ballroom dancing had to do with an AA meeting, but I figured I'd find out later. So I went back to the ship and changed clothes so I would look a little nicer for the evening. When 5:30 p.m. rolled around, I left the ship and walked down the pier and across the street, where the hotel was. The restaurant was in the front of the hotel. As I walked in, I looked around and saw a giant dance floor and a few people sitting in a booth. There was an older couple in formal wear who noticed me as I walked in. It must have been kinda early for dancing because, being the only ones in the restaurant at the time, they were easy to recognize; and so was I. They waved me over to them and asked me if I was the one who called, then they moved over so I could sit down. After telling them my name, they introduced themselves to me.

I still couldn't figure out why I was there if they were just going ballroom dancing, because it was obvious they weren't going to have a meeting. But I figured out later that that was just a way so I could be with people who didn't drink, and it helped, and I didn't feel lonely anymore. A few more people came in and sat in the booth next to us, and they all seemed to know each other, so I felt like I was at a meeting there at the restaurant. Then the waitress came over, and we ordered dinner, and afterward, I watched them dance. When the evening was over, they told me that the next day they were going to an English-speaking meeting in another city about fifty miles away. They asked me to meet them there at the restaurant in the same place at nine thirty in the morning, as this was a noon meeting we were going to. I agreed and couldn't wait till the next morning. I went to my rack (or bed) in anticipation of the next day.

Morning came, and when I woke up, I went back to the hotel and waited in the booth for my new friends. I got there early enough to have some breakfast before they came in. When they finally got there, we went outside, and I got in the car. I noticed it was a rather small car, but I squeezed in with five other people. We started driving down the side streets, and they said, "We have one more person to pick up," but I couldn't figure out where they were going to put him in the car. When we found him on the corner, I realized it was a homeless man. They opened the hatchback, and he lay down in it like he'd done this before. As we were leaving town, they told me that he knew five different languages fluently. It showed me that no matter how smart you are, anybody can become an alcoholic. As we were driving farther away from town, I was looking out into the beautiful countryside of brown grassy fields and a few rolling hills as this was a pretty dry climate. I can see why the British make this their vacation spot.

A little over an hour after we left, I could see our destination in front of us. Living in the United States, I have never seen anything like it. It looked like a giant wall in front of us with windows in it, and it had a huge wooden gate where the road ended. It opened up as we went through, and I noticed it was an ancient walled city built into a square. We pulled up to the inside of one wall and parked in front of it where there was a door. We all piled out of the car and went inside where there were a lot of chairs set up in a big circle. Even though it was an English-speaking meeting, I was amazed to hear people from different parts of the world like Northern Ireland and even one person from Russia coming together with a common bond, a common disease called alcoholism. I was so glad I could be there. After the meeting was over, we drove back to Palma de Mallorca and said our goodbyes.

Chapter 23
Life on the Riviera

The next morning, we set sail for Southern France or the French Riviera. We pulled into port at a city called Toulon. The captain invited a few of the crew, about thirty of us, to go out on an excursion that was designed to be a dedication to rebuild a castle. I don't know how, and I couldn't believe it, but I was handpicked to go with the group. We took a bus through the foothills of the French Alps, which was in the province. It was a beautiful ride through lush green forests till we got to the base of a castle that had been taken apart for hundreds of years by the locals, rock by rock. That was why we were there, so they could possibly put the castle back together again like it was in the beginning.

When we arrived at our destination, they had a nice picnic area set up for us near the castle. We had a guide who spoke a little English show us the castle and what they were doing to try to rebuild it. I happen to have an English-French translator book with me, and I used it even though I took two years of French in high school, but I wasn't very fluent. The French like to drink, of course, so all the picnic tables had a bottle of brandy in the middle of them with bottles of wine lined up on each side. By this time, I wasn't really tempted to drink. I met a lady there, though, who wasn't drinking either because she said she was driving herself and her husband home and couldn't drink. Her name was Yvette, and her husband's name was Georges. We spent the day trying to communicate with each other, and I was sharing my English-French book with everyone too. I had a lot of fun even though I wasn't drinking, and we were all sharing our clothing with the French also. I gave my hat away to somebody. By the end of the day, everybody, except me and the captain, was drunk, something I think the captain noticed; and nobody had their regular uniforms on. This was very embarrassing, but the XO (or second-in-command of the ship) got so drunk he passed out under a tree, and they had to carry him onto the bus. It seemed that I wasn't the only one who had a problem with alcohol because that was only the first of many drunken escapades he had on the cruise. Later on, he kept coming back to the ship drunk, and he had to be taken off the ship and sent back to the States. What a way for an XO to lose his career. Maybe he'll be put in rehab like I was. You never know.

Yvette and Georges just happened to live in Toulon, so I got their address to go visit them when we got back. The next day after work, I decided to leave the ship and go out and look for Yvette and Georges's apartment house. They said they didn't live too far away because Georges worked on the base. It was exciting to walk down the narrow streets looking for someone I knew in a foreign country. As I walked downtown, looking for their apartment house, I noticed down one street a marketplace, and I was surprised to see they let dogs run around loose everywhere, and they didn't even get upset if they're inside the market where the food was either. It's such a relaxed atmosphere. That's what I like about the French. I kept walking, and I discovered an open square with a beautiful fountain in the middle, and there was a person dressed in a black-and-white clown suit on the sidewalk doing a mime. It was just like I've seen on TV. After watching the person doing the mime, I showed one of the other spectators the address I had on the paper, and they gave me some directions. Motioning with their hands, they showed me how to get there.

I kept on walking down the narrow streets, and I finally found the apartment house where the address was. I entered the apartment and walked up the stairs to the third floor. When I found the apartment number and knocked on the door, Yvette cracked the door open and saw me standing there. She was happily surprised that I had successfully found their place. I could tell by the smile on her face, and she immediately invited me inside where I was welcomed by a white miniature French poodle, named Bill. They told me later that they liked Americans so much that they named their dog Bill. I was tickled by that. Georges was sitting down reading his paper at the time. They introduced me to their teenage daughter named Magdalene. I brought my English-French translator book with me, but it was an interesting evening trying to communicate with them.

They invited me to stay for dinner; and after we ate, they told me to wait while they called a girl, who lived downstairs, to come up and translate for us. Her name was Denise, and she was in the French Army and knew how to speak English quite well. At the end of the evening, I invited the whole group to come out to the ship, and I would give them a tour. They said they would come out the next day after Denise and Georges got off work. I said my goodbyes and told them I would meet them after work the next day.

The next day, as I was giving them a tour, I met Captain Wright, and he told me he was impressed because he couldn't get any of his visitors on the base because it was a "closed base," but because Georges worked on the base and Denise was in the French Army, they were able to get on the base and see the ship. Denise and I hit it off pretty good, and she told me to come to where she worked at the hospital, and she would give me a tour of Toulon. So the following day, I went to her workplace, and we walked up to a tramway that took us up the side of the mountain that overlooked Toulon. It was so beautiful. At the top, I was surprised to see that there was a zoo that had giraffes and bears and other animals. It was amazing. After we were done looking at the animals, we went down the tramway and back downtown and to the market to get bread and food for the dinner that she was going to fix for me that evening at her apartment. I wasn't lonely anymore. In fact, I had made friends in a foreign country and felt right at home with these beautiful people who had adopted me.

One day after work, I decided to go to an AA meeting. I found it very difficult not knowing the language when I was getting on the bus, because the bus driver was irritated when I was trying to get directions. At the same time, he wanted me to give him the exact change so I wouldn't interrupt his timely schedule. So once I sat down, I asked the lady next to me and showed her the address, and she told me what stop to get off and where to go from there. Once I got off, it wasn't hard to find the church since it was right there on the corner. I walked inside and saw it wasn't a very big room with a rectangular table and chairs all around it, but it was big enough for the few, about eight to ten people, who came to the meeting that night. I noticed the placards on the table with "Live and let live" and "But for the grace of God" and "Think, think, think," all in French. But I could understand exactly what they said since we have the same thing at our AA meetings here in America. I didn't say much during the meeting, and when I did, I had to look at my English-French translator book to say anything. Then, right after the meeting, a couple came up to me and asked me if I wanted a ride back. I was surprised to hear them speak to me in fluent English, and they sounded like Americans. I only wished they had said something to me in English during the meeting, but it was all okay. And they took me back to the base where I got to my ship and went to bed sober. A few days later, we left port and headed for Italy. I was sad to leave my friends, but I knew I had to go. I never saw or heard from any of these people ever again, but they will remain in my heart forever.

CHAPTER 24

ON OUR WAY TO ITALY

First stop—Genoa: We found out we were headed for Genoa, which is the birthplace of Christopher Columbus, and we happened to get there just in time for his birthday. It was raining as we pulled into port, greeted by a whole bunch of elementary students waving American flags; and we came in appropriately wearing dress whites, manning the rails. Since it was the first time an American ship pulled into Genoa in twenty years, that made it even more special and why the grand reception. It felt proud to be an American that day. After we pulled in, I asked two other females and Jessup, a big black guy who worked with me, to go see the Leaning Tower of Pisa. So the next day when we were all off duty, we took a cab to the train station. The rain had stopped, and it was a beautiful day to take a train ride across the country to Pisa. When we got there, we walked downtown to where the Leaning Tower was. It was surprisingly uncrowded on the streets as we made our way to the tower. As we were walking up the stairs, I was amazed how the whole thing was made of stone, and the stairs were worn smooth because of hundreds of years of people walking up them, but because it was made of stone, it was so heavy. That's what caused it to lean. The first three stories had no railing on the outside, but the upper three stories had just a thin metal railing, made of iron, and you can walk around the outside. I heard later that people have been known to fall off the edge of the first three stories. While we were there, we heard of a schoolchild who fell off the edge of the third story and died just a couple weeks before that. We walked around the square and went into some of the other buildings and saw the beautiful ceilings that Michelangelo had painted. We had lunch there in an outdoor restaurant, and afterward, we got on the train and went back to the ship in Genoa. The following day, we left port and headed for Gaeta, Italy, which was further south along the coast.

Second stop—Gaeta: Gaeta is a small port city that was known for Carnivali time. After dark, as we walked along the waterfront next to the seawall, it was like a circus, all lit up with food vendors, souvenirs, and hand puppets. It was perfect, watching all the families having fun, especially the little children.

When we got there, we were moored across the pier from another US ship, the *Belknap*. This older American ship that was stationed there year-round was in need of a lot of repairs, and that was our job. By this time, I knew my craft pretty well and, because of my rank, was made supervisor. The first-class petty officer in charge told me to go over to the *Belknap* and find out what kinds of repairs were needed. I went over and talked to the engineering officer, and he had one of his seamen show me down in the engine room and fire room (or boiler room) what kinds of repairs were needed, and I found out it was quite extensive. One of the rooms had a lot of gray tape wrapped around the piping, and I was told to pull it off before they could work on it. I was working, for at least a couple of hours, pulling off the tape and breathing in the dust, until the safety officer, Lieutenant Bradington, came in and told me that it was asbestos. She asked me why I didn't have protection on, and I told her they never told me it was asbestos. When I went back to my ship, I asked them why they didn't tell me it was asbestos, and they said, "Well, you would have done it anyway."

I said, "Yeah, but with protection on!" They didn't care. Next, I was told they needed to see me on the mess decks of the *Belknap* for a pipe that needed repairing. As I was waiting on the mess deck, I had a cup of coffee, and a sailor came in and showed me the pipe and pulled off some of the insulation, and it started leaking. So I called the pipe shop on our ship to come and repair the pipe so we could replace the insulation after they were done. It took at least two months for us and the pipe shop to complete the repairs on the ship.

I made sure no one tore any more gray tape off the pipes unless they were wearing protective suits and masks.

After we first got there, when I got a day off, I went ashore to find a lady called Margo, who was the drug and alcohol counselor on shore and happened to be married to one of the sailors on the *Belknap*. She was a British lady, and they also had a little boy named Ethan. I found her office so I could find out where some AA meetings were. She said there weren't any English-speaking meetings in the area, but that was okay. As long as I was in her company, I felt safe. We spent about three months there in Gaeta; and on my off-duty time, I got to go to the beach quite a bit on the other side of town, which was beautiful. The beach was lined with lounge chairs, and all you had to do was sit and relax by the water, and a waiter would come up to you and ask what you wanted to drink or eat. I never knew how delicious cappuccinos and expressos were until I got there. It was definitely a paradise.

Most of the time, I went out by myself exploring, and Margo told me about taking a tour with a group to a mission on top of a place called Split Mountain. Starting out at the base, it wasn't very steep at first, and we went down a trail that led us between two rock walls on each side about forty feet high (that was where it was split). On one side, there was, what looked like, a handprint in the solid rock wall; and they told us that "when Jesus died on the cross, the mountain split in two, and He was there and put His handprint into the side of the wall." I put my hand into His handprint, and they told me, "You can feel the power of Jesus by doing that." As we kept on walking, I looked up and saw a natural archway above us, which we walked underneath. Then we started climbing up the hillside on the trail, and when we got to the top of the mountain, there was a small mission building with a statue of Jesus overlooking the ocean. It was a beautiful view. After looking at the mission and the statue, we started walking down the trail, and we kept walking down and down into this cave where it was getting darker. And as we kept walking down, it started getting lighter in the cave, and then we started to hear water and waves crashing. The farther down we got, we could see a big opening at the bottom, which opened out to the ocean. It was big enough for a small boat to come into the cave. As we got to the bottom, there was a small beach; and unless you had a boat, we realized we had to go back the same way we came in. You definitely had to be in good shape for this tour.

While we were still there in Gaeta, Captain Wright got a group of fifty sailors together to take a bus tour of Rome and a papal audience at the Vatican. I'm not Catholic, but it was exciting to be within five feet of the pope as he walked by us, and I took some pictures of him. Unfortunately, the pictures got lost in Hurricane Charlie in 2004 with all the other pictures I took while I was in the military.

Third stop—Naples: We left port for a cruise along the coast of Italy down to Sicily, and as we were leaving, we were told that our battle group was going to Australia. We all got excited thinking we were going with them, but we were told that our ship wasn't needed and had to stay behind in Italy. As I was topside, enjoying the beautiful day and taking in the view of the islands as we were cruising by, I could see in the distance that there were some low-hanging wires in front of us connecting the islands between Sicily and Italy. As we got closer, I wasn't sure if the mast of our ship was too high or not to fit under them. I was right. The wires were too low, and the mast was just a couple of feet too tall. As we got closer, I got more and more worried we weren't going to make it; and suddenly, the captain came over the loudspeaker and announced, "All hands, brace yourselves, because we are going to list [or lean] the ship over to one side so we can fit under the wires." So Captain Wright, with his navigational skills, turned the ship so it would lean over just enough so we could fit underneath the wires perfectly. It was an amazing thing to actually watch. After we made it under the wires, we sailed around the southern tip of Sicily and moored offshore.

We weren't allowed to go ashore, and that's where we found out that the battle group was going to go to Australia without us. We only spent one night there, and the next day, we set sail for Naples. We sailed around the other side of Sicily so we wouldn't have to go under the wires again. We made it to Naples later that day, and as we pulled into port, I couldn't help but notice the trash in the water around the piers. We heard it said that Naples was the armpit of Italy.

It definitely wasn't as clean as Gaeta. But then I noticed something even more gruesome: a dead rat floated by, followed by a dead cat. Before we got there to Naples, I heard stories that there were dead babies in the water sometimes. If I hadn't seen the dead rat and cat, I wouldn't have believed it.

Since I had the following day off, I made a plan to take a train ride up to Gaeta to see Margo. Nobody wanted to go with me, so I went out by myself. Everybody else said they were going out sightseeing, but I know they were going out drinking, and they just didn't want me to go with them as usual. That morning, right after muster (7:00 a.m.), I got out of my uniform and into my civies (civilian clothes) and started walking downtown to the train station; and as I got to a corner intersection, I asked a gentleman who happened to be standing there, "Do you speak English?"

He said, "Yes, I do, a little."

I asked him, "Which way to the train station?" He pointed down the street and told me how to get there, and then he asked me, "Are you English?"

I said proudly, "I'm an American."

And then he said, unexpectedly, and in a derogatory voice, "Americans!" and spit on the ground. That not only scared me, but also made me realize that not everyone in Europe likes Americans, so I started walking away as fast as I could in the direction he told me. As I looked behind me, I noticed that he was following. Thank goodness I wasn't too far away from the train station, and as I got there, I noticed a couple of Italian police standing at the gate, so I motioned to them in a way they could understand that the man coming behind me in the distance was following me, and asked how I could get away from him. They then pointed to a stairway that took me underneath and to the other side of the train so I could elude him. I told them in Italian, "Thank you." When I went to the other side of the train, I looked back, and I never saw him again. I got on the train and sat down, and when I looked around, I didn't see him, so I felt pretty safe.

After another lovely train ride, I got off and took a cab to Margo's office downtown. She was surprised, but happy to see me. It was just about lunchtime, and she invited me to come with her to her house for an early dinner, but first, we had to pick up her son, Ethan, at the day care. Then we stopped for some seafood at a seaside market. When we got to her house, she baked up some mussels and clams with garlic and lemon sauce on them. I never had mussels before and never again tasted as delicious as that. After that enjoyable visit with her and her son, she drove me back to the train station, and I took the train back to Naples and walked back to the ship with no more incidents. We only spent two days in the Port of Naples (because our captain only liked nice ports), and then we headed back up to Gaeta to finish our work with the *Belknap*.

Chapter 25

Back to Gaeta

Toward the end of our stay in Gaeta, which was a couple of months in all, I went over to the *Belknap* to check on the status of our repairs, and the engineering officer stopped me and asked, "What's your name, sailor?" When I told him, he wrote it down on a tablet.

I asked him, "What's wrong?"

He said, "Nothing, I'm so impressed with you guys getting everything done plus what was done on the mess decks, which was added to the list, that I want to recommend you for letter of commendation." I felt proud, but I didn't think I was doing anything special because I was just doing my job.

I went back to my shop happy with the job that we finished, and as I walked in, the first class of the shop, having some paperwork in his hands, asked me if I had some coffee on the mess decks, and I said, "Yes, I was waiting for the pipe shop to come and fix the pipe." Then he asked me if I got some sodas out of the soda machine, and I said, "Yes, I was getting sodas for the crew," and I asked him, "What's wrong?"

He said, "I have to put you on report."

I said, "What for?"

He said, "I took your evals [evaluation report] to the division officer, which I gave you 3.8 [4.0 being perfect] and highly recommended for advancement, and he took the evals and ripped them up right in front of me and told me he wanted you busted, and he didn't care how, so I'm writing you up for dereliction of duty." I was shocked, to say the least! I couldn't believe what my ears were hearing. I thought after all these months of proving that I could not only do the job, but also run a crew of men as well as the next man and get everything done, the division officer could see that I was a good sailor and worthy of being promoted, not demoted! I knew that he was bound and determined to make sure not just me, but all women weren't allowed on ships. Fortunately for other women and the progress of the armed services, he and other men (old salts) like him were getting too few and far between. A day later, I was sent to the captain's mast.

I didn't know what to do. All I wanted to do was give up, and immediately I thought of a drink, though this time it was different. I looked for someone I could talk to, and the first person I ran into was Jessup. I just blurted out, "I want a drink!"

He asked me, "When was the last time you called your family and talked to them?"

I told him, "About a week ago."

Not having cell phones at this time, he said, "Let's go ashore and call on the pay phone."

I said, "Okay, that sounds like a better idea." Thank goodness I got a hold of my husband right away, and when I talked to him, I told him what was going on and that I wanted to drink. I usually didn't confide in him about my drinking, but this time I let him know everything, and I'm glad I did. He told me that he (the division officer) wasn't worth drinking over, and it would just put me in more trouble. So I agreed with him and told him I loved him, and after saying our goodbyes, I went back to the ship.

Chapter 26
Captain's Mast

The next morning at muster, right after we were excused, the division officer came up to me and told me I had to go to captain's mast. He told me to immediately go and put my dress whites on and meet him up in the office next to the captain's stateroom and be there in the next thirty minutes. I walked downstairs to get dressed, and as I was dressing, I felt different. I wasn't afraid anymore. I knew I didn't do anything wrong, and I didn't deserve to be treated the way I was. I didn't really care what was going to happen to me.

I walked into the office, and I looked around and saw the command master chief, the command chaplain, and the division officer all sitting down and Captain Wright sitting behind his desk facing everyone. Since I was the accused, I had no chair and was made to stand up. For the first few minutes, there was complete silence; and then the captain said, "What's this all about?"

Trying to discredit me, the division officer immediately said, "This petty officer has never worked in her rate the whole time she's been in the Navy."

The captain then said, "What's that got to do with anything?"

For the first time, not having any fear in me, I blurted out, "This all started when I first got on board and Petty Officer Bradley asked me out, and I refused because I was married, and then it escalated from there to sexual discrimination by the chief, and I was made to work nights and put on report for not finishing jobs that couldn't be finished, and when I showed that I could do the work, the division officer put me on report for getting coffee on the mess decks and getting soda out of the soda machines for the men! And I have worked in my rate. In my first enlistment, I worked in sheet metal and disaster preparedness."

Suddenly, the command master chief asked me, "Did you write your congressman?"

I said, "No, I didn't. My husband wrote our congressman." Thank goodness he (the captain) got to know me and what kind of work I'd done. Captain Wright had a mission when he came aboard the ship, and that was to integrate women on his ship. And he knew the division officer was going against him by trying to keep women off ships.

So after I was done talking, he said, looking the division officer right in the eyes, "I don't want to hear any more about this! You're all dismissed!"

The next day, I went to the chaplain, and I asked him why he was there. He told me that they, the command master chief and the division officer, had it planned to put me on charges of conspiracy against the command for writing my congressman and that they were going to have me busted and put out of the Navy. After I heard that, I sat there in shock. I didn't feel like drinking, but I felt like giving up. I was so angry, all I could think about was getting even and shooting everyone. I had it all planned out that the next time I got the quarterdeck watch, I would take the .45 pistol; and I would take hostages, like Petty Officer Bradley, Chief Rodinez, and the division officer, Chief Warrant Officer Murdock, and shoot them and push them over the end of the ship and watch them get churned up in the screw (or propeller), seeing their blood and guts discolor the water around. My mind was consumed with those thoughts constantly, and I would go to bed every night thinking about that. Fortunately for them, I never got the quarterdeck watch again or had a gun in my hand after that.

CHAPTER 27

ROTA, SPAIN

The following morning, we left port and headed toward the Straits of Gibraltar and out of the Mediterranean Sea. Our next stop was Rota, Spain, before heading back to the United States. We met the rest of the battle group at Rota and planned to stay there for just two days before heading back. During the whole trip, I tried to get an AA meeting started, but nobody would show up. I figured I was probably the only one on board trying to stay sober or in the program Alcoholics Anonymous. I had a couple of friends I could talk to and helped me, like Jessup, but still nobody would show up for the meetings. After the captain's mast, I pretty much gave up on holding meetings, but I found out there were a couple of chiefs on another ship who were in the program, just in time for us to go out on liberty in Spain.

As we got together on the pier, they asked me if I knew how to horseback ride, and I said I loved horseback riding. I knew this was just what I needed to get my mind off my problems. We walked across town, and I noticed that while this was lunchtime, everything was very quiet because everybody was taking a siesta. I thought it would be nice if the whole world would take siestas. We finally got to the stables that were near the beach. As we mounted our horses, we walked them down to the beach and into the water. I've always wanted to ride horses on the beach, but to ride a horse across the beaches of Spain was something you could only dream about. After an hour of riding up and down the beach, we made it back to the stables and headed back to the ship. I didn't want the afternoon to end, but I knew that we had to go back.

While we were parting company at the pier, I thanked the chiefs immensely for helping me get through a very difficult time and said goodbye as we went to our respective ships. God knew this was exactly what I needed because after the captain's mast, all I felt like doing was to lie in my rack and be depressed. I didn't even want to go to work from then on. The next morning, I was watching television in the female lounge; and all of a sudden, the person on watch in the quarterdeck, sounding very shaky, came over the loudspeaker and said, "General quarters, general quarters, all hands, man your battle stations. This is not a drill! There is a lube oil leak in the fire room! All hands, this is not a drill! Man your battle stations!" This was exactly what we've been training for since I got aboard. I didn't have my boots on, but I've never put my boots on and climbed up the ladders and out of the berthing area faster since.

Running as fast as I could, I got to the entrance to the fire room in a matter of, what seemed like, seconds; and I met the assistant on-scene leader. The on-scene leader, or "the one in charge," was supposed to be there, but he was on leave, so that meant that the guy I was meeting was in charge, or the "on-scene leader," and I was the "assistant on-scene leader" at this time. As we got our helmets on, we looked at each other; and I asked him, "Now what do we do since our leader isn't here?"

He said, "We'll do just like we always practiced before. You get the hoses down and connected together, and I'll light off the A-FFF station" (which is a fire retardant foam that fills up the fire room or the engine room as needed). After I got the hoses down, my hose team started showing up, one at a time, and I got them organized by telling them what to do, just like we practiced over and over again. And now we were ready for anything. A "lube oil leak" is no minor thing, because if the lube oil mixes with anything electrical, it could lead to an explosion, which could destroy the ship and cause it to sink. And that's why acting fast is important so that everything could be soaked with foam before it could catch on fire. Well, the foam did it, "kept everything from blowing up." As I was standing there over my hose team, I noticed the chiefs and officers starting to show up; but all they could do was watch, as we had everything under control. If you'd have timed this, it would have been the fastest ever, but I guess adrenaline will do that.

Well, we cleaned up our mess, and they fixed the leak, and we were ready to leave the following morning for home. I was still refusing to work and staying in the berthing area watching recordings on the television because, of course, we couldn't get any reception out at sea. I was depressed and feeling sorry for myself, but I felt I had a right. If I had been using the program of Alcoholics Anonymous, I would have been going on with my life and learning not to have resentments, which is the number one offender, which causes people to drink, especially me. I wasn't hurting anyone but myself with my pity party. AA has taught me, since then, to pray for those that I hate the most or have a resentment toward. It really works, but unfortunately, I wasn't using the program because I wasn't going to meetings to learn enough of the program at that time.

CHAPTER 28

BACK TO THE STATES

The next day, we left with the whole battle group to get home to Norfolk, Virginia. It wasn't as smooth seas as going to the Med, but it was a lot quicker getting home. I was topside, when a week later, as we were getting close to home, the battle group, which was about seven destroyers, separated themselves from us; and as they got farther away, they were all in a line and blew their cannons off as a salute to us for a job well done. Our captain also let us know over the loudspeaker, "Thanks, and job well done from the battle group." It was a very proud moment to witness.

Since I got on the ship and all during the Med cruise, I had been going to Lieutenant Bradington, the head nurse and in charge of female morale, to talk to for the sexual harassment and eventual depression I was going through. I didn't know that she called back to the States about my captain's mast and told a Lieutenant Commander Haskins about my plight, who, in turn, went to the vice admiral about it, and somehow, *60 Minutes* got wind of it, and they all met us at the pier when we got back to Norfolk.

It was in midafternoon as we pulled into port, and we were met by the vice admiral who made our ship the staff ship. The *60 Minutes* bus was there on the pier, and I was standing at the rail watching Mike Wallace get off the bus with all his entourage. Suddenly, two male sailors took me by the arms and escorted me about five decks below to a little cubbyhole of an office to work. I was taken out of the repair department and put in the supply department called ROVSS (Repair of Other Vessels Supply Support). I heard that the division officer handpicked three female sailors to be interviewed by *60 Minutes* so they would cover up the story of the harassment I went through. I never got to talk to anyone about it.

There was a chief in charge of the shop that I was working in, and he could see that I was depressed, and he told me he knew why. He said, "I saw what you did during general quarters, and anyone else would have been given a medal, but because of who you are and the enemies above you, you will never get recognized for what you did. You have to remember, you did your job and saved the ship from blowing up, so don't worry about working right now. You can just sit there and read as far as I'm concerned until you're ready to go to work." I couldn't believe what I was hearing, but he knew that I was depressed, and he understood why.

When I went home, I decided to take a thirty-day leave of absence. I was a lunatic to my family. My poor daughter caught the brunt of it because I went into her bedroom and saw that she hadn't cleaned it for probably the whole four months I'd been gone. Because I was such a perfectionist, I was full of anger, and I lashed out on both my husband and my daughter. So I decided to take a drive, and as I was driving, I got to the freeway and stopped at a rest area and called them back and told them I was going to Florida to visit my parents. I only took my purse with me, nothing else. I drove for hours, and nine hundred miles later, I got to my parents' house, and then I realized I had to go to the store and get a bathing suit so I could take a dip in the pool and a nightgown to sleep in overnight.

The next morning, I woke up and drove home. All I wanted to do was get away or run away, which helped a little bit. I was somewhat calmer when I got home. We celebrated Christmas, and I was still angry and depressed. Then New Year's Eve came, and yes, I wanted to drink. But for some reason, I knew that it was not an option anymore, and I thought about my daughter and how much I would hurt her if I drank. So instead drinking a beer, I had a cup of Nyquil and went to bed. That was my last drink, and even though it was a medicine, I still count it as my last drink, because I didn't have a cold, and it has a lot of alcohol in it. I started my sobriety date on January 1988.

After I went back to work, I started learning quite a bit about the computers and what my job entailed. We were in charge of ordering parts for the ships that we were repairing. It was a new job and very challenging, and I started to really get into it and love it. There was a first-class petty officer working there also, but all he did was sit in the corner and sleep. After a couple of weeks, I started feeling like I had some hope of redeeming myself, especially since I didn't see that division officer anymore. A few weeks later, I was put in charge of expediting parts for supply, which meant I had to take a van outside the base and go up about fifty miles away to get parts from other bases, or storage areas, including the weapons station near my home. It made my job a lot more interesting and outgoing. Unfortunately, after the captain's mast in Italy, I started cultivating a resentment of the worst kind. All I could think about was the next time I had the quarterdeck watch, I was going to use the .45 pistol and take the division officer and the others who hurt me hostage. Then I would shoot them and throw them off the aft end of the ship and watch them being churned up in the propeller, blood gushing in the water. The Lord knew better because I never had the quarterdeck watch or touched a pistol again after that.

CHAPTER 29
GOING CRAZY

After working at ROVSS for about a year, I got a letter that said my grandmother died. Then, at around the same time at work, when I was expecting a better evaluation report, especially after working as well as I had been, I was told that the division officer ruined my career; and I would never make advancement again. He gave me 3.2 and not recommended for advancement on my evaluation report. I didn't realize the anger and resentment I had boiling inside me was about to run over, and I suddenly snapped! If anyone got in my face, I wanted to kill them, and I would literally scare people by throwing tantrums like a little child. I was so full of anger I just couldn't control myself. I was immediately sent to the VA hospital in Portsmouth, where they evaluated me and kept me for a few nights on observation. I was put on a medication called Haldol and sent back to work on the ship. I couldn't seem to concentrate. All I wanted to do was write down how I felt, which is what the doctor wanted me to do, but not while I was working. I was working for a commander in her office, and when she told me to do something, all I did was write. So I was relieved of my duties and sent home. Pretty soon I was mustered out of the Navy with an honorable discharge but not able to reenlist.

Right after I got out of the military, we were pretty hard up for money. We didn't have any income except for what Ollie was bringing home, as he was crabbing off the shores of the Chesapeake Bay with a friend from church. It was a bad year with slim pickings, and they only made about $25 a week doing that. We were about seven months behind in our trailer payment, and I got sued for having cable television that we didn't pay for, so we owed $1,000 for that. Ollie was paying the bills, and he said we never got a bill for it since we had the cable put in our house. In court, I told the judge that all we could afford to pay was $5 a month at the time, and they accepted it. We were going to church in a little town called Guinea where Ollie's friend lived. The VA hospital told me I couldn't work because I couldn't handle the stress, so I volunteered at the Salvation Army as a secretary, but that's all I could do, mentally.

One Sunday, we went to church, and I went up in front of the church and asked for prayers because of our financial situation. Afterward, I went home and got down on my knees. I was scared to death, but I looked around and told God that He had given me a roof over my head and food on the table up till that day. And then I told God that I would not get off my knees until He took away the fear of financial insecurity. I didn't ask for riches. I just wanted the fear to be gone. All of a sudden, I felt a warmth around me like a blanket or someone hugging me like the time after I got drunk and almost died. Then I felt a peace, and all my fear went away. Then I promised to tithe, from then on, no matter how much money I had. I got up feeling much better, and a couple of days later, I got a check in the mail from our income tax, and then I got a check the next day for my disability. I wish I could say I never have fear of financial insecurity again, but I have never missed a payment for a bill or been without enough money to live on since then.

God knew that I needed to get out of the Navy and off the ship, because not quite a year after I got out, a piece of sheet metal came loose and fell on exactly the same spot in the passageway where we used to muster in the morning and killed three sailors, two men and a woman. That would have been me if I'd still been there. For fourteen years, I was on so many medications, but none of them agreed with me. I would wind up in and out of the mental ward at the VA hospital in Hampton, Virginia. At first, they told me I couldn't get disability because I was born that way with a personality disorder. I decided to fight it, because I spent my first four years in the Navy with good evals and even reenlisted, so how could I be born that way? I finally found the right counselor who asked me if I had any documentation on what I had been through, and I told her, "Yes, I documented everything." So I brought all my little notebooks with names, dates, and times in to her; and she typed it all up and sent it to Washington. I finally got my disability of 100 percent. That was 1994.

It took another two years to get declared totally and permanently disabled. But I couldn't stand the way I felt. I was constantly losing my temper and wanting to commit suicide. I was angry all the time, especially at my daughter, but I didn't drink. I would get angry and smash my fist through the wall, and I would slam the doors so they would break. Eventually, my daughter got pregnant in high school and left home and later got married. I don't blame her for leaving. She was only thinking of the safety of my granddaughter. One time I even got so angry at my husband that, while he was sleeping, I put my hands around his throat because I wanted to kill him. He suddenly woke up with a shocked look in his eyes, and he's a big man too. I would end up in the hospital every month or two, sometimes for up to thirty days because the medications they would try just wouldn't work or would have terrible side effects.

One time they put me on a medication that made me want to drive ninety miles an hour along narrow winding roads, and then I wanted to see what it was like to be handcuffed by police, so I drove to the freeway. I saw a cop car going the other way, and I did a U-turn and tried to follow him. Then I realized what I was doing and went straight to the hospital where they admitted me immediately. I was lucky I didn't get arrested or killed in a car accident. They would just switch my medication to something that was stronger and tell me that I was immature. They put me on so much medication that I don't remember two years of my life. They were experimenting by giving me a drug especially made for veterans with PTSD. It was called the forgetting drug.

One day, I had an eye doctor appointment at the new VA that was just built, and when I went in, they told me that I had been there six months earlier, but I told them, "No, I was here three years ago at the old hospital, but I have never been to this new hospital."

They said, "You're right here in the computer." They also told me I was on a certain medication that made me forget, but I just couldn't believe it. I had stopped taking it a couple of months earlier. It was like I was in a blackout for two years. I prayed every day that I could get off all medications.

Chapter 30
The Cure

This was the beginning of a series of miracles that only a Christian could see. One night, I met a woman in AA and asked her to be my sponsor. She told me she didn't usually sponsor people on medication, so I decided to quit taking all my medications. Then about the same time as I was walking in my backyard, I got a tick stuck in my right arm. I asked Ollie to pull the tick out with a pair of tweezers, and he squeezed it, and it pushed the poison into me. My whole arm swelled up, and I started feeling hot and sweaty, so I went to the emergency. They sent me to the VA, and they tested me for Lyme disease, but it came back negative. Not knowing whether it was the tick bite or getting off the medications, or both, I went home and started throwing up every day for thirty days. I didn't eat, drink, or sleep for thirty days. I was sweating profusely and even hot and cold at the same time. I went to the emergency twice for IV fluids, and they wanted me to go back on my medications, but I refused. I couldn't hold them down anyway. So I went back home and couldn't eat or drink and kept vomiting every day.

Toward the end of thirty days, I must have been hallucinating when I saw two deer, two rabbits, and two groundhogs outside my front window at the same time, just walking around eating and enjoying themselves. I was just lying there on the couch watching the whole thing. It was in the country, so it could have been real. To this day, I'm still not sure. Then I saw on television a mother quit giving her kids gluten, and I wondered what gluten was. The kids were autistic, and they started acting better and responding better to treatment and not as many angry outbursts. I started reading up on gluten, and a lady at the bowling alley gave me an allergy magazine. A doctor, inside the magazine, said that gluten acts as an opiate on your brain if you're sensitive to it. I found out that gluten is a protein in wheat. So I didn't eat gluten for another month, which was a total of sixty days without gluten; and then one day, I had some pancakes, just to see what would happen. As I was driving down the road, I noticed my head felt like a band was tightening up around it, and my eyeballs felt like they were going to burst. I tried to smile, but I couldn't. I just wanted to be angry. That was the answer to my mental disorder. If I stayed away from gluten, I could be normal or sane.

One day, I just wanted a piece of pizza, and nothing really happened right away. Then I had a second piece, and I wanted to kill the dog, so I ran to the bedroom. Then I wanted to throw the television off onto the floor, so I just shut the light off and sat on the edge of the bed rocking back and forth. I told my sponsor how I felt, and she finally admitted that it wasn't just an alcoholic personality. It was a mental problem caused by an allergy to gluten. After that, I started working the twelve steps of Alcoholics Anonymous with her. I drove to her house, fifty miles up the coast, every Sunday after church, to read the Big Book with her and a few other girls. By the time a year had gone by, one by one, the other girls dropped out; and I was the only one left. I had done the steps and not only purged my conscience, but also took responsibility for my actions and my feelings and was so much better mentally than I had ever been in my life. I learned the power of forgiveness. It was the beginning of a new life of not only sobriety, but sanity as well. It has not been a bowl of cherries, far from it, but it was like coming out of a fourteen-year coma. I felt alive for the first time with no desire to drink.

When I went to rehab, I remember after each counseling session we would say the Serenity Prayer; and at the end of the Serenity Prayer, we would also say, "Grant them health, prosperity, and happiness." For the full six weeks I was there, we said this, not knowing why we were saying it and who we were saying it for, until the very last day when our counselor said, "You all were praying for the ones you hate the most." I realized I was praying for him, my counselor, because I hated him after he said he was a profound atheist. At the time, I didn't understand anything about spirituality, and I hated anyone who didn't believe in God. What a hypocrite I was just because I proclaimed to be a Christian.

Since then, I have used that prayer many times, and it has worked every time. Either the person has been taken out of my life or they became my best friend. As an example, when I worked for the chief at my first duty station, SIMA Mayport, one of the jobs I had was just going around the shops and getting signatures. I thought it was the most boring job in the world, but it wasn't just that. The chief I worked for hated me, probably because the captain gave me that job and even promoted me to E-5 when I bowled for the Navy. No matter what I did, he found fault with everything. After enduring that for just a few weeks, I started praying for him and saying to myself, "Grant him health, prosperity, and happiness," over and over again. All of a sudden, one day he asked me to come into the office with him, and all I could think about was *What did I do wrong this time?* He looked rather disgusted and perplexed and proceeded to explain to me that I had been promoted to another job working with the chiefs as a planner, planning out the jobs for the ships and ordering the parts for the pumps. I was shocked. I didn't understand why I was being transferred, but it was the best thing that happened to me in a long time. I thought it was because of what I prayed for, but like I said, every time I said that prayer for someone, they were either taken out of my life or became my best friend.

Unfortunately, I wasn't using that prayer when I had my nervous breakdown, and that caused me to become so resentful that all my hate went inward, and I lost just about everything, including the Navy, because of it. For about a year, I couldn't eat very much like gluten or wheat products, but I couldn't even eat eggs or beef or even drink coffee, because it upset my stomach and made me feel like I was going to heave. I lost a total of thirty pounds and kept it off for a long time. I finally asked the doctor at the Hampton VA to take out my gallbladder because I felt like it was poisoned from the tick bite, and they told me no. So I asked for a second opinion, and they sent me to the VA hospital in Richmond, Virginia, where the doctor there was willing. After the operation, it took a while, a long while, but eventually, I was able to eat better, but I still stayed away from gluten.

CHAPTER 31

THE HURRICANES

After getting my disability, Ollie and I started volunteering for the Disabled American Veterans. He became a commander of that chapter, and I was a chaplain. It really kept us busy. We had a neighbor who was a congresswoman named Joanne Davis who was such a good advocate for the veterans and came to some of our meetings. She would insist on my sitting next to her up front. She became my best friend. While we lived in Virginia, it seemed like we were going through a lot of hurricanes because we were right near the coast on the Chesapeake Bay. For two years in a row, we had Hurricane Bonnie and then Hurricane Isabel. We didn't really lose anything except power; but it was so inconvenient, being without power or water for two weeks after Hurricane Isabel, that I just wanted to get away from the hurricanes by moving to Florida to be near my family. When I told Joanne we were moving to Florida, she called me a traitor for moving but gave me a big hug goodbye, and that was the last time I ever saw her again.

I figured, where we were moving to, Arcadia, Florida, was inland, far enough to keep us safe from the hurricanes; but boy was I wrong. So pretty soon I felt well enough to move to Florida to be near my father who was alone after my mother died. My sister Mary moved to be near him also with her son, my nephew, Jamie. We all lived in the same small town, and my younger sister lived in Tampa. It was so nice living near my family, at least some of them, for the first time in my life since I left home after high school. Before we moved, we decided to buy a motor home and go down to visit my elder sister in Florida, especially since we had two boxers, and they would fit in the motor home just fine.

After being there a few months, we found a mobile home on half an acre and decided to buy it. We moved in on May first, 2004, and on the Fourth of July, we had a family reunion and a house-warming party, but just the day before, the air conditioner suddenly exploded, sending sparks and flames in the air. Needless to say, it was in the '90s, and everybody got hot, and my family went home early instead of staying the whole week. Then we got a portable air conditioner, and it leaked water through the floorboards, which was horrible because those older mobile homes used pressed cardboard for flooring. Then the ants invaded the master bedroom, and we had to call the exterminators. They sprayed in the mobile home, but it didn't do any good because they were coming in over the tree limbs onto the roof and into the house. I told my husband, "I would like to throw this mobile home away and put in a new one." Later on I realized, "Be careful what you ask for because you might get it."

Friday, August 13, 2004. They were tracking a hurricane in the Gulf that we thought was going to Tampa, but suddenly it turned into the harbor in Punta Gorda. My sister Mary's husband had passed away, and she inherited a twenty-eight-foot boat and was living on it in the boatyard in Punta Gorda. So I called her and asked her where she was going to stay during the hurricane, and she said she was going to stay in Dad's garage. Because they didn't take pets at the Turner Center, we were going to stay at home, but I agreed to bring the two boxers to stay with her and Dad in the garage. Ollie and I drove both the car and the pickup over to Dad's house, which was a mobile home, but pretty sturdy because it had additions built onto it. Once there, in the big two-and-a-half-car garage, I set up chairs around the minivan, thinking we could sit down and enjoy ourselves while the hurricane was outside. As the hurricane got stronger, the roof started shaking up and down, like it was going to blow off; so we all jumped into the van except Dad because he refused to come out of the house and into the garage. I was sitting in the driver's seat, and I noticed a big tree outside the garage had pushed its way through the roof and was coming down onto the front of the van.

Ollie yelled, "Get the dogs in the front and get to the back of the van!" It didn't push all the way down, but praise the Lord, that tree kept the roof from blowing off completely. All total in the minivan, there were my husband, Ollie; my sister, Mary; our two boxers, Romeo and Juliet; her chow and her two big parrots; and me. During the middle of the hurricane, my sister got upset and was crying because Dad wouldn't come out of the house, so I told her I would go see if I could get him to come to the garage. When I tried to get out of the garage, I couldn't get the door open because of the suction of the wind. I was finally able to open the door and run across the lawn next to the swimming pool, which lost its pool cage. When I got to the door of Dad's house, I looked back and saw I had just run over power lines. Thank goodness the power was off at the time or I would have been dead. God again was looking over me. I looked in the house and saw it was dark and thought maybe the house was caved in, so I went back to the garage and told my sister. With her head in her hands, she started crying uncontrollably, saying, "Dad! Dad!" I told her I would go back and check again. I went back, and this time I pushed the door of the home open, and my dad came out of the bedroom and asked, "What's wrong?" I told him that Mary was upset and wanted him out in the garage in the van with us. His words were "Just tell her I'm taking a nap," and went back into the bedroom. Being a WWII vet and eighty-nine years old, I wasn't about to argue and went back to my sister and told her what he said.

After the winds had died down, we went outside to assess the damage. We had a tree fall on the cars but just scratched them up a bit with no real damage, but we couldn't get out of the driveway because of the tree branches all over the car and the truck. So we went next door to the Mennonites and asked them if they had any chain saws to get us out, and as we stood there talking in their driveway, we noticed two cars totally crushed and flattened, and I asked, "What happened to them?" They pointed to a cement slab in the middle of the field behind their place, and he said, "There used to be a shed big enough to house a semi in it, but the empty shed rolled over our cars." It actually ended up against my dad's fence.

They finally cut us out, and we drove our cars back to the house or what was left of our house. When we got there, we saw that the motor home sitting in the driveway in front wasn't even touched. The sides of the mobile home, where the awnings were, had been pulled out and away from the house. The awnings were meant to save the house, but the winds went underneath and ripped them and the walls away from it. There was only a corner of the roof left over the living room to cover my mother's electric piano that I inherited from her. And the back bedroom had a roof over it to cover my Star Trek collection in plastic crates and my husband's stationary bicycle. All I found was one gold medal out of three golds and a bronze that I won in 1984, bowling for the Navy. It was a miracle we didn't stay at the house because the Turner Center (the local shelter my aunt and uncle built) didn't accept pets, and we were going to stay home because of the dogs. We would have died for sure. I'm just glad I called my sister and found out where she was staying. We took the piano to the neighbor so he could keep it until we could get a new mobile home put in. We built a shed in the backyard and put everything we could salvage in that.

We wanted to stay in the motor home, but it was ninety degrees, and we didn't have enough gas for the generator that ran the air conditioner, so we had to take the motor home to Bradenton, the nearest town, for gasoline. When we got there, our transmission broke down, so we had to get a motel. It seemed like we were hit with one problem after another. And I thought I had been through a lot before that, but life seems to hit you when you're not expecting it. The funny thing was, I never thought of a drink even going through all this. I was an emotional mess though, and I even cried a lot. We stayed a week in a hotel while our motor home was being fixed, and during that time, we went to the Red Cross to get help and met a man there who sounded exactly like Wolfman Jack. He had a radio station in the sixties and seventies and was known for his really gruff voice. We came to find out he was Wolfman Jack's voice double when he had throat cancer and did his show for his last fourteen years. This is what he told us. He also told us he had a radio station around the corner and asked me to talk on it about the hurricane, which was an experience I'll never forget. After we got our motor home fixed, we had to evacuate the area because of another hurricane, Francis, and then later, Hurricane Jeanne. It was definitely the year of the hurricanes.

We decided to head up to Michigan; and just past Tampa, on I-75, we were in a huge traffic jam with a long line of cars and trucks pulling horse trailers and other motor homes like ours pulling our vehicles behind. It was the biggest exodus since the Israelites leaving Egypt. I was still traumatized by the hurricanes, and every time I opened the Bible, I would open up to Job. God knew I needed to read that. I started reading the Bible at that time, and I've read it almost ten times through since. When we got to Tennessee, where my daughters-in-law lived and we held family reunions, Hurricane Francis was right on our tail following us. We spent one night and left the next day for Michigan just before Francis got to us. After we got to Michigan, we heard that it headed for Canada only as a tropical storm. We stayed and visited with Ollie's kids about a week and then headed down to Gloucester, Virginia, to visit friends there and where we went to church when I got out of the Navy. We stayed a few days in the church parking lot; and then we headed to Savannah, Georgia, to be near my daughter and her husband and our granddaughter. We stayed in a mobile home park, and that was to be our home for the next few months, till we got a new mobile home set up in Florida.

My mother died in 1999 of breast cancer, while we were still living in Virginia. I drove down to be with her in her final days. That's why I needed to move to Florida, so I can be near my dad. Also to get away from the hurricanes, but that was a mistake. It was nice being close to family for the first time since leaving home. I had my sister, my dad, and my nephew, who was like a brother to me when I first moved to Michigan in 1972 living in the same small town.

CHAPTER 32
NEW HOME

After we got settled in the new mobile home, my husband went in for a routine catheterization, but it was anything but routine. This was because he was still recovering from a stroke he had in Virginia, which effected his left side; but by this time, he was doing remarkably well. Just some weakness. While I was waiting for the procedure, I was reading my Bible. Suddenly, the doctor came in and said they have to redo the catheterization because his artery ruptured on the first procedure. I prayed and told the Lord I wasn't ready to be alone yet. He heard me because they did emergency surgery and put in two stents, and he lived through it.

After we got settled in our new home, my friend in AA invited us to his church, which was a small building in a cow pasture. It happened to be right around the corner from my dad's house. Because of that, my dad started coming to church after the minister visited him. It was so nice having my dad at church with us. My sister went to a church that was very strict, which I was the type I was baptized in when I was eighteen. After I got sober, I didn't want to go back to that church. They believed that musical instruments don't belong in the church and women are to be silent in church also. In other words, only the men could teach and lead singing. I was told by my sister's ex-husband, who was an elder, that this was the only church going to heaven. What a judgmental attitude I had because of this teaching. After rehab, AA taught me to be tolerant of other people's beliefs and to open my mind to other types of churches, and that's why I believe

God led me to this church. It was similar to my sister's church, but we have musical instruments and a choir I can sing in.

When I was getting sober, my sponsor told me not to go to church for a while because I was confused about God. I couldn't understand why God didn't just fix me and my addiction and why he let all those bad things happen to me, especially when I knew the Bible and I thought I had faith. Since then, I have learned that knowing or believing in God and having faith are two totally different things. It's also not what church you go to, but the personal relationship you have with the Lord, Jesus. After a few months of going to church with my dad and my husband, I noticed my dad losing weight. He was already a thin man, but he started looking like skin and bones. Then one day he told me he passed out and fell off his bicycle. He was always very active and athletic. On his seventieth birthday, he went out running with my younger sister, who ran marathons, and a while later, she came back tired, but he didn't come back for a half hour. Then he jumped in the pool and got on his bicycle and went back out. Now he's ninety-two, and he's been riding his bicycle over twenty miles a day. I knew this because I saw him riding his bike about ten miles from his house just before this happened. After he told me about passing out and when I saw how thin he was, I knew something was very wrong. Then I went over to his house and asked him to come live with us.

The first night he collapsed, and we took him to the hospital. He had a seizure, and they transported him to Sarasota Memorial Hospital. The next day, they planned to do an endoscopy to see why he was throwing up all the time. It was to be the next day at 10:00 a.m. I got there at ten in the morning, and he was in, having the procedure early. I didn't even get to say goodbye. As I was waiting, it was apparent that something was very wrong. Nurses were running through with the crash cart. It was so sudden I didn't know what to think. Out of five kids in our family, I was the only one there taking care of him, and I felt very alone. After giving them written orders that I had a power of attorney and a DNR (do not resuscitate), they resuscitated him twice.

Unfortunately, he went into a coma. For two days and nights, I stayed by his side, alone. I finally had to tell the doctor to unplug the respirator. When his heart finally stopped, I shut his eyes with my fingers and knelt down by his bed and cried. I was so loud they had to shut the doors to his room, which was in the cardiac ICU. Later, I had to be the executor of all my parents' possessions, which was horrible because I was still grieving and emotionally drained. I'm so glad my brothers and sisters were as supportive and helpful as they were. Nobody really complained about what they got. I promised Dad before he died that I would make sure it would be divided evenly. My brother did get some property and a life insurance, but I realized later that he really earned it. He did help raise my sister and me. After all the times he took us water-skiing with his boat and even taught me to snow ski by taking me up to the top of the highest ski lift and leaving me there. I learned the hard way.

A few months later, I got a call from my big sister who moved to West Palm Beach to be with her daughter. She was screaming on the phone so much I couldn't understand her. She finally cried out, "Jamie is dead!" I drove to her son's house, who lived with his three kids less than a mile away. As I walked into the living room of his house, the EMTs were bringing his body out on a stretcher. I started crying as I stroked and kissed his forehead. He had diabetes, and just before this day, he was struggling with his wife leaving him and taking care of his children by himself. On top of this, he also lost his job because of losing his eyesight to diabetes. He was a truck driver. Thank goodness one of his sons got his driver's license. The other son was mentally disabled, and he had a beautiful daughter as well. They would come over to my house a lot. I wanted to help him when his wife left, but I had enough to worry about with my husband and my dad. It was overwhelming, to say the least. Then I became tasked with finding homes for his kids to live. They each went to a friend's house till the end of the school year. Then their grandfather in Alabama came and took them home with him.

CHAPTER 33
ANOTHER MOVE

After losing my dad and my nephew, and my sister moving to the other side of the state, it definitely wasn't the same as when I moved to Florida to be near my family. Because of Ollie's heart condition, we decided to move to Port Charlotte, about thirty miles away, to be near the hospitals. Living in Arcadia, his heart doctors were in Sarasota about forty-five miles away. It was a smart move. We even bought a house between two bowling alleys. That was a big plus. I didn't realize the impact the stress had on me, with all that I had been through and the moving as well.

Right after getting settled in, I went to the bowling lanes on a Saturday to try coaching the kids. I went to the bathroom, and when I leaned over the sink to wash my hands, I felt the most excruciating pain in my lower back. I went right away to the chiropractor, and he saw some red spots on my left hip. He immediately said, "I think you have the shingles." I've had friends who had the shingles, and I know they were in a lot of pain. Well, now I know how they felt because I could hardly move. It was a paralyzing pain in my lower spine that kept me in bed for months after that. It was coupled with the pain of loneliness I haven't felt since I got sober. We just moved from Arcadia after losing my family. Even my church family, who was about thirty miles away, never came out to visit me. I just got a new sponsor in AA whom I called almost every day, but when she asked if I needed her to come to visit, I got the feeling she really didn't want to, so I said, "No, I'm fine." Just like an alcoholic, too much pride to let her know how lonely I was.

The thing I did do was to pray a lot. I noticed I never had one single thought of a drink, and I hadn't had that urge or compulsion for a long time. I believe it was taken away when I did the twelve steps with my sponsor up in Virginia. I just kept the thought of what Jesus went through on the cross for me. Thanks to AA, I also made a gratitude list every day so I could keep a positive attitude. I memorized some scriptures like "I can do all things through Christ which strengthens me" (Philippians 4:13). Also, "My God shall supply all my needs according to his riches in glory by Christ Jesus" (Philippians 4:19). By this time, Ollie started sleeping in the other bedroom because every time he touched me, the pain was excruciating. So I was even sleeping alone for the first time since I left the ship in the Navy.

This was a time I started memorizing Bible verses. My sister sent me a poster. I still have it above the door in my bedroom facing me in my bed. It's a bald eagle soaring above the trees and the scripture Isaiah 40:31, "But they that wait upon the Lord shall renew their strength; they shall mount up with wings as eagles; they shall run, and not be weary; and they shall walk, and not faint."

I have learned that the more hardships I go through, I seem to get closer to the Lord. I have noticed sometimes others have the opposite effect. God gives everybody a choice. We can either get stronger, if we don't die, or have a lot of self-pity and become weaker and drink over it. Staying sober has definitely made me stronger.

I wish I could say this was the end of all the pain and hardships for the rest of my life, but of course it wasn't. It's like after getting sober and doing the steps, life should become a bed of roses. Right? Wrong! You don't get stronger by sitting around not doing exercises. I've found that out in my life.

After moving to Port Charlotte, of course I joined a bowling league, or two. Unfortunately, Ollie had to quit bowling because of his knees, but he went with me to watch. We even volunteered for a senior hospital program in running a league. Little did we know we'd be running it for the next eight years. I also volunteered for Meals on Wheels for the same length of time, from 2008 to 2015. There was a ninety-year-old man I admired so much volunteering with me as a driver. He even bowled in the league with me. He would pick up those containers full of food like they were nothing and put them in his car. He was a wonderful Christian man, small in stature but so big in his earnestness for the Lord. He wore a big cross around his neck, but he didn't need it to show he was a Christian. His actions spoke for himself.

I learned to volunteer when I got out of the Navy because I couldn't work at the time, and it helped keep me sober. I encourage my sponsees to do the same. That's really how the AA program works; it's called doing service work. Not only did it keep me busy so I didn't think of a drink; but it taught me not to worry about money and to depend on God for everything and to pray more, which I did, but not as much as I do now. I'm finding I'm still growing, even today with my praying. It took me literally years to worry less about money because of my impulse buying. I'd usually buy something like a car or a house and completely forget to pray and ask God what he thinks I should do. I had to have it no matter what. I eventually learned to pray that he take away my wants and desires so I could live at peace with less anxiety and be grateful with what I have.

When we moved to Arcadia and bought a house, or mobile home, my sponsor up in Virginia asked me why I didn't consult her about the house. I thought she was just being controlling, and I thought I was an adult who could make my own decisions. I learned later, a lot later, that even though I am an adult, I don't make the best decisions, but this has been the way I've lived all my life, and it's hard to change. I have found out that I'm not the only one who can't stand change. At least changing my behaviors. Alcoholics are the worst. Like I said before, I'm still learning; but as long as a stay sober and open minded and willing, it's getting better, much better. After getting over the shingles, I wish I could say I never went through any more pain; but the Lord must have figured I could handle not just more, but a lot more.

After moving to Port Charlotte, I started bowling better than I ever did. My average went up to the 190s, and one year my highest average was 217. I figure being sober and not on medication has a lot to do with it. Thanks to a lady who ran the 500 Club, I got to travel around the state and even the country bowling in tournaments. She was a great organizer. We went to Reno more than anywhere for the women's nationals. I had a lot of fun even though I don't really like to gamble. To me, bowling is not gambling; it's based on skill, and I feel God gave me that gift, and I give him credit for it. One time we got to go to El Paso for the nationals. In my entire bowling career, starting before I enlisted in the Navy, I have been to eight or nine nationals, including the queen's tournament at Niagara Falls, which is a professional tournament. Bowling has given me a fun and wonderful life to look back on.

Unfortunately, it has taken me years later to learn forgiveness and understanding it better. You would think that after working the fourth and fifth steps by the book (the Big Book) with my sponsor up in Virginia, I would understand the reasons why I was treated so badly by the chief and division officer on the ship, but I just couldn't figure out what I did wrong or if I did anything wrong at all. It took me years to realize or to take responsibility for what my part was or what I did wrong. What did I do to provoke them to treat me the way they did? It all boils down to fear. When I got to the ship, I may have had almost two years of sobriety, but I hadn't worked the steps yet, and I didn't go to a lot of meetings. I was full of fear and hardly any faith to speak of. Not even praying much at that time either. I left myself vulnerable to be the victim again. I don't give them the excuse to do what they did, but in the Navy, in order to make rank, you have to prove you're a leader, and I sure as hell didn't act like one. When I got to the ship, because of fear and not working the AA program, I was an E5 but acted like an E1. Eventually, after about a year and a half, I got more of a backbone; but to the division officer, it was too late. I already proved my unworthiness.

When I first got to the ship, my chief ordered me to swab (mop) the deck in front of the E1s or subordinates. So I did, fearing that I could be busted if I didn't obey orders. I didn't think about handing the swab over to the nearest E1 and delegating that job like a good E5. I know now, years later, I was probably being tested because there was another E5; and one of us was up for the job of shop supervisor. I actually had seniority, but he wasn't going to give it to a wimp like me. I eventually lost my sense of fear when my resentments grew so big I wanted to kill everybody. All my anger inside me grew every day after that captain's mast, which led to my nervous breakdown. I learned in the alcohol rehab to pray for those I hate the most, which I didn't do then when I needed to, but since working the steps, I've been praying for them, and now I honestly forgive them.

I also learned to forgive those who beat and raped me and left me in my van to burn up in Michigan the same way. What was my part? I was a drunk. I also learned to forgive myself because I now know that I was a sick person with a disease of alcoholism. Not a bad person like I thought I was, and I'm learning to take responsibility for my actions.

In 2010, because of a dump truck accident we had in 2001, I had to have surgery to replace two discs in my neck. Right before we moved to Florida, we were on our way to the bowling alley in Gloucester, Virginia, in our pickup truck. We were just going through the light that turned green when a dump truck, fully loaded, going about fifty miles per hour, hit us broadside. It hit the rear of the truck, or Ollie would have been killed, and spun us around. Instead of going to the hospital to be checked out, we must have been in shock and thought we were fine, so we went bowling. After bowling, Ollie said, "My side hurts."

And I said, "Yeah, my neck hurts too." So we went to the ER, and after some x-rays, they said Ollie had two broken ribs and also put a neck brace on me. We didn't know it, but this accident would affect our health, especially in the latter years of our lives. That's why I had to have my neck surgery. A couple of other people in my church had the same surgery, and it went well with them, but it didn't go so well with me. After I came out of anesthesia, the muscles in my left arm and shoulder were so cramped, I was crying. It was horrible pain. The doctor couldn't figure out what was wrong. I had to go in for x-rays to find out. They said I had bone spurs pressing on the spinal cord. I didn't want more surgery, so I had physical therapy and a great massage therapist who calmed the muscles down with deep tissue massage. I figured that was the end of that and got back to bowling right away.

Later in 2012, I had foot surgery in my push-away foot in bowl-ing. That pain was so bad I even broke a chair when I was convalesc-ing at home. It finally got better, and I was able to bowl again. Then for three years, the VA was watching my left kidney and my thyroid because I had tumors in both. I had three small tumors in the right side of my thyroid and a huge one on the left side. They kept saying they were all too small to worry about, but for about a year, my left side had a strange ache in my lower back. I blame all these tumors on a job I had right before I enlisted in the Navy.

I was delivering radioactive hospital supplies around the state of Michigan in a small Pinto wagon. I would pick up the boxes at the airport right across the street from where we lived, then I would put warning signs on my car saying, "Radioactive Stay Away." I then drove all night to hospitals and universities. The people coming out to get the boxes would always be dressed in protective suits. A few weeks after I started working, the company finally gave me a lead shield to hang on the back of my seat and a pin to detect how much radiation I accumulated. By this time, it was a little too late. My hair was falling out in big clumps. Then they hired a man and made him my supervisor and even paid him more money. That was a kick in the gut, since I was the first one hired. He said it was because he had a family to provide for. So did I, but that was downright sexual discrimination. That was a big reason why I joined the military. I wanted to be the breadwinner and not depend on a man anymore, even though I loved Ollie. So I quit, but I'm sure all my tumors were probably because of that job.

As I was saying, three years after the VA noticed my tumors, my VA doctor got sick and sent me to an outside doctor for my thyroid first. I immediately had surgery, and he removed the left side of my thyroid, but he said it was so large he couldn't believe I could still swallow. Thank goodness it was a benign tumor. Not cancer. Then a few months later, I had gone to a kidney specialist and had a pro-cedure done called an RFA (radio frequency ablation). In a one-day surgery, they inserted a needle in my back and into the kidney and burned the tumor out. They did a biopsy, and it took a couple of months to get the results because the VA insurance cancelled all my future appointments. I just assumed it was like my thyroid and was benign. I finally got a hold of the doctor, and he told me it was a malignant carcinoma or cancer, but he was sure he got it all. A month later, I bowled in an invitational tournament for 150 of the highest average bowlers in southwest Florida. It had eight games, and after each game, we had to move to the next lane, which was a lot of work. After the fifth game, a young man in his twenties, bowling next to me, said he was exhausted because he wasn't used to bowling that much. I said, "Well, I'm almost sixty and surviving kidney cancer, but I'm still feeling pretty good." I came in fiftieth place, which I thought was excellent. Second place out of only three women bowlers. Unfortunately, I had to be in the top 25 to bowl in the next round. It was fun anyway.

I was hoping that the kidney was the last surgery, but I know that life isn't always predictable. A couple of years later, my left arm would be numb when sleeping. I thought I was just pressing on a nerve in my neck. Then it went to both arms. When I had the neck surgery for the two discs replaced, they said I had a bone spur pressing on my spinal cord. I went in to the VA to have an MRI, and the results were much worse than a bone spur. It was another tumor wrapped around my spinal cord at the base of my neck. I found a neurosurgeon in Cape Coral who has done the surgery at least thirty times. The VA approved at first. So I scheduled the surgery for January 3, 2017. I was a substitute teacher that year.

In December, as I was at the high school, I checked my phone after working with a student; and my husband, Ollie, left me a message that he was on the floor and couldn't get up. I called my neighbor, Rob, right away to go check on Ollie. He didn't look that well before I left that morning, but he said he was okay. I told the regular teacher I was helping that I had to get home right away. He understood since he was a caretaker for his wife also. When I got home, Ollie had collapsed between the chair and his scooter, and Rob and I couldn't get him up, so I called 911. They came, and they got him in his chair but said Ollie had a high temperature and needed to be hospitalized. When he got to the hospital, he was put on the heart ward. At first, I didn't understand why but found out that he had another heart attack with a urinary tract infection, plus he had pneumonia. I stayed with him for over twenty-four hours and held him down while he was delirious. I thought he was going to die, and I started praying. As I was holding his arms down so he wouldn't pull out his IVs, I looked up and saw the figure of Jesus standing over him. It looked like He was weeping too. I wanted to ask Him if Ollie was going to die, but He just disappeared. I think He was letting me know He was with me and I wasn't alone and He was feeling my pain. Our pain.

Ollie suddenly calmed down, so I decided to go home to take care of the dogs. Thank goodness the Lord provided us with the best neighbors who took care of our little Chihuahuas for us while we were gone. I came back the next morning and found Ollie doing better and out of the heart ward. He seemed to be doing better when suddenly he started having a seizure. They called the crash team in, and a stupid nurse who looked like she should be at home with her grandchildren started talking to me about Ollie like he was sure to die. I told her to get away from me because she was an idiot. I don't know what she was thinking. But I walked away and started praying again. I didn't see Jesus this time, but they got him stabilized, and he just acted like he didn't have a problem. That's Ollie for ya. Well, he was there on Christmas and his birthday, the day after Christmas. I baked him a cake, and the nurses and I gave him a nice little party. The next day, he was sent to a rehab center.

On January 3, my sponsor took me to Cape Coral Hospital for surgery. The day before the surgery was scheduled, I got a call from the neurosurgeon's nurse telling me that the VA's insurance cancelled the surgery. I couldn't believe it! Then about five o'clock, I got a call from the surgeon himself telling me to come into the emergency room, then they could get me ready for the next day as planned. My sponsor and another sponsee drove me down right away. She came back the next day and stayed with me after the surgery. She was an angel sent by God. After the surgery, I spent three days in the ICU. A room by myself. I couldn't lie down flat on my back even to sleep for the next three weeks because they had to cut into my spinal sheath to take out the tumor, and they didn't want any spinal fluid to leak out afterward. Because they ripped the muscles on the back of my neck, the pain afterward was excruciating. As I was kinda lying upright in my bed, crying from the pain, a lady came into my room and said she was a chaplain to deliver a prayer blanket. It was a knitted shawl. I still have it to this day. She helped me by reminding me to meditate on thinking nice thoughts. It didn't take the pain away, but just having someone to distract me was nice.

On the third day, I had to call my congressman because the VA insurance refused to pay my bill. I also had to find a ride to the rehab because the VA refused to transport me. They said the reason was because it was out of the county. But it was where Ollie was at. I had to go from Cape Coral to Port Charlotte, and they didn't have an ambulance, so they found me a transport van. When I got to the rehab, they had to get Ollie's roommate out so we could be in the same room together. It was a bit sketchy at first, but it turned out perfect. Thanks to my faith, I knew God would take care of everything. And of course everything worked out fine. For three weeks we rehabbed together. The nurses would snicker when I would push Ollie in the wheelchair down the hall to the dining room, saying, "Isn't that a cute couple." We finally got discharged together to go home.

Picture with husband ollie

My praises go out to my neighbor for taking care of our dogs, even walking them every day. Only God could have provided someone like that. Other people would see all the negatives through all these (what I call situations), but I see it as life on life's terms and a lot of positives to put on my gratitude list. I've found out it wasn't just the surgery that was hard to go through, but my goal afterward was to get back to bowling, which I thought would be difficult, but my whole life has been difficult. It just took longer, and my health will never be the same. Six weeks after the surgery, it started with a light ten-pound ball and only one to two games. Then eventually, about a year, I got back to my twelve-pound ball. Then after three years, the beginning of the season, I picked up the fourteen-pound ball I used to bowl with when I had a 217 average. It's been about seven years ago.

With the physical therapy I have been doing almost daily since the surgery, I started throwing high 200s again and 700 series. I felt great again. But I found I needed to read up on bowling psychology, because every time I had about eight or nine strikes in a row, I would go crazy and get totally nervous. Then at the same time, I started praying for a 300 game, and I promised I would give all the glory to God. The week I finished the book, the night before bowling, I hemmed a new shirt with my church's name and a big cross on it. As we were practicing for the league, one of the other team members said to me, "You are going to have a 300 game against us today." I just smirked but didn't say anything because I was thinking he just jinxed me.

Then another one of their team members said, "Yes, you are going to have a 300 against us today." I kept thinking the same thing, but I didn't say a word. The first game was all strikes but two spares. Then the second game I started out striking. What's weird was that this little old lady had a chair on the approach because she couldn't go up and down the step, and that's where she sat. Normally I would get nervous or insecure when someone was right behind me, especially talking to me, but this time I would go up and bowl a strike and turn around and give her a high five. She would say each time, "Good going. Keep it up."

Years before this, I had a counselor who gave me a mindful meditation tape I used it almost every day, which helped with my breathing; so every time I sat down, I would try to think about my breathing. On the last ball of the game, I tried to think of it as being just another ball and not important or how quiet the bowling alley had gotten with all eyes in the building on me. I picked up my ball, like every other time, grabbed my towel, and wiped the excess oil off my ball. Then I took a deep breath and threw the ball. It rolled down the lane right on the same mark where I had put it each time before, but this time it looked like the 10 pin (the right corner pin) was about to stay standing, but it fell. I fell too. On the floor. I collapsed because this was my first sanctioned, perfect 300 game. I made them in practice before but not in league or tournaments. I turned around, and the manager was taking my picture for social media. I looked up and pointed to the cross on my shirt and gave God the glory. It was kinda funny because others in the bowling alley wore their "church shirts" for weeks after that. I guess they wanted a perfect game too.

After starting bowling at thirteen, it took me fifty-one years to finally accomplish that, and I thought my bowling days were over after my back surgery. Because the Lord has given me the gift of sobriety, I made two of my bucket lists that year, 2018: the perfect 300 game and making the USBC (United States Bowling Congress), Southwest Florida All Star Team. Now, because of the COVID-19 virus, I'm staying home with my wonderful husband, who put up with me all these years and my two dogs, who keep me busy, and because I turn my will and my life over to the Lord every day and thank Him every night, my life couldn't be better, no matter what the circumstances. I only wish others, who battle with addictions or alcoholism, could get the same assurance that if I could get through my life and be happy, joyous, and free, as I am now, anybody can do it with a little faith, "one day at a time."

Oh yes, I've mentioned seeing some famous people face-to-face, along the way, in my lifetime, and they were: two presidents, Queen Elizabeth, the pope, the Sasquatch (or bigfoot), and the most famous of them all, Jesus.

Dedicating My Book

First I want to dedicate this book to my sister Bonnie, who prayed for me all my life and I don't think I would be here today if it wasn't for her. Then to all my sponsors in AA. To my first sponsors who have gone into heaven Bert and Jack, just one of a number of husband and wife teams who were there when I needed them. To another team, when my ship was in the yards, in Baltimore, who gave me my first Big Book, Bill and Betty. To Michelene and Elvis. To Connie and Barriman, who also have gone into heaven and I know I will see again someday as fellow believers in Christ. To Lauri, who passed away due to cancer, the one who helped me through the twelve steps by the book. To Alice, after moving to Florida but also passed away from cancer soon after. Jennie, who helped me through my father's passing. And now my present sponsors, Idell and Forest, who I hope will be with me for a long time to come. I also want to dedicate this book to my daughter, Sunny, who I put through hell before and after I stopped drinking. And of course my husband, Ollie, who I love so much, and has stuck with me no matter what. There are so many others that I can't list them all but I know I couldn't have gotten sober all by myself. That's why God gave me AA. Thank you Lord.

ABOUT THE AUTHOR

This is a woman whose life was shaped by the men and boys whom not only she grew up to admire but also whose footsteps she hoped to walk in. Her father never treated the girls in the family different or let them believe they couldn't do things because of their gender. Her brothers were also a big factor in her life. Not only did she have mixed feelings of wishing she were a boy, but there were many more challenges with growing up in a military family such as moving around and making friends, which was hard for her. She could blame all this on her problems with trying to escape into alcoholism, but later, it might have made her stronger and given her more desire to turn to the Lord. Either way, her faith and the fact that God didn't give up on her show that the example of the mustard seed is very true. Thank goodness for that.